So, You Want to Live on an Island ...

Charles + Susan
Cecilia +
    Micheala.
Thanks for
coming to see
us. Enjoy
    Gary

So, You Want to Live on an Island ...

Gay Morse

EDITED BY CLAUDETTE UPTON

WITH ILLUSTRATIONS BY JUDY STEELE

© 2004 by Gay Cokendolpher Morse

Publisher's Cataloging in Publication Data

Morse, Gay
    So, you want to live on an island ... / Gay Morse
        p. : ill.;   cm.

ISBN: 0-9749556-0-4

1. Little Cayman Island (Cayman Islands) – Humor
2. Travel – Cayman Islands – Little Cayman – Diving
I. Title

The West Indian is not exactly hostile to change, but he is not much inclined to believe in it. (This comes from a piece of wisdom that his climate of eternal summer teaches him. It is that, under all the parade of human effort and noise, today is like yesterday and tomorrow will be like today; that existence is a wheel of recurring patterns from which no one escapes; that all anybody does in this life is live for a while and then die for good, without finding out much; and that therefore the idea is to take things easy and enjoy the passing time under the sun.) The white people charging hopefully around the island these days in the noon glare, making deals, bulldozing airstrips, hammering up hotels, laying out marinas, opening new banks, night clubs and gift shops, are to him merely a passing plague. They have come before and gone before.

—Herman Wouk, *Don't Stop the Carnival*

Contents

Author's Note

All of these stories are true. They have been donated by people who live in the islands and people who have traveled to islands. Some of the people wanted you to know their names, and others preferred to remain anonymous. The names that have been changed are footnoted, with the reason indicated at the bottom of the page.

So, you want to live on an island ...

At some point in their lives, most people dream of quitting their stressful jobs and humdrum existence to run away to a carefree, romantic island. This book is dedicated to those who actually followed through on the dream—and never went back to "normal" life. It is especially dedicated to divemasters, who, day in and day out, create a comfortable environment for guests on vacation.

If you have ever worked with the public (and haven't we all, at some time!) you can appreciate the humor it requires. Some of the stories in this book may sound twisted; for those who live and work on an island, however, a twisted sense of humor is the first requirement, *before* your expertise in whatever field you have chosen to work.

So ... if you have ever wanted to live on an island, or if you have already lived on an island, this book has been written for you. Its intent is to bring a smile to your face and stir some fond memories. I have tried to include something about people in many walks of life, since the blending of cultures, personalities, and quirks is what gives the spice to life in the islands. I believe this is why people return year after year ... to escape from the norm. Grab a hammock and a piña colada, and enjoy!

Gay Cokendolpher Morse

Introduction

This book started as an idea back in 1985, when I moved to Grand Cayman to be a divemaster/scuba instructor in the Caribbean. Over the years, visitors would laugh at the stories we told on the dive boat. One comment I heard repeatedly was "You should write a book ...". I don't claim to be a writer; in fact, the funny stories practically tell themselves.

Many of these stories could have happened on any island ... or anywhere people travel. We are all tourists when we travel to a new destination. In fact, just so you know that I'm writing this book to show the funny side of traveling and not making fun of people, I'll share a personal story.

My husband, Ed, and I were married in 1990. As a wedding gift, his mother gave me a beautiful safari dress and Ed a handsome bush jacket for our honeymoon in Africa. We had hired a private guide so we could travel alone and not be bothered by other tourists. Since our work revolves around the day-to-day dealings of a small Caribbean resort that caters to people's needs, we needed this time alone. One of the first days out, we were dressed in our special Africa outfits for our day photographing wild animals. As we entered a small village, our guide pulled to a stop in front of a tiny store so we could buy extra drinks to carry with us in the bush. When we stepped from the car, imagine my husband's horror (he *hates* being a tourist!) when a group of African children playing in the street pointed at both of us and screamed repeatedly "Banana Republic! Banana Republic!" At that moment, I realized that, wherever we go ... we are all tourists.

Some years later, after hearing over and over again how lucky I was to live on an island, and how this person and that person wished he or she could quit work and go live on an island, I decided to write this book. In many ways, living on an island is great. But ... before you quit your job and relocate, you should read this book. It will show that there is a lot of repetition in our days. The names may change, but the stories remain much the same.

What *is* important is a sense of humor. The people who survive and actually thrive on island life have that twinkle in their eye and see the humor in an event even before the event takes place. You learn to expect the unexpected. It's harder to get things done here ... but the view is worth the trade. So ... if you're still interested ... read on!

A geographical note: Grand Cayman is the largest of the three Cayman Islands. It is known for beautiful Seven Mile Beach, great restaurants, duty-free island shopping, the Turtle Farm (which breeds and raises sea turtles), submarines, and nightclubs. It has it all. When you go to Cayman Brac, you immediately sense "small community" and realize you can leave your watch at home. "The Brac" has accessible land caves, a high bluff overlooking the ocean 140 feet below, a Parrot Preserve, and only a handful of places to stay. You unwind very quickly there. Little Cayman has five dive resorts, each with its own personality. All the resorts dive the famous Bloody Bay wall (weather-dependent, of course). In the afternoons, people cycle around the island, nap in hammocks by the sea, go to the only grocery store, or watch iguanas basking in the sun. Though the Caymans are famous for their banks, the bank on Little Cayman is open only one day a week! You definitely feel you are a part of a unique, small, friendly community in Little Cayman.

1

Cruiseship Madness

One of my all-time favorite stories revolves around cruiseships. Of course, after a couple of years of dealing with cruiseships, I chose to move to the more remote outer island of Little Cayman. But I'm getting ahead of myself...

It was a beautiful sunny day in the Caribbean, with flat seas, which was a blessing, considering our mission. We were to go on our 52-foot dive boat to George Town Harbor to pick up cruiseship snorkelers. We had already taken scuba divers out for two dives, then dropped off the divers, stripped the boat of scuba equipment, and converted it to a snorkeling boat prepared to carry fifty to sixty passengers (average age sixty-plus) to three different snorkeling reefs.

To get the full visual impact, you must realize that there are three boats, each carrying fifty to sixty neophyte snorkelers, alternating on three shallow reefs. The staff on each boat is responsible for teaching the people to snorkel within the two-hour time limit and returning to the harbor with the same number of people we left with. Good luck!

As we motor past the huge cruiseships anchored outside the harbor, the same questions get asked and answered by the divemasters each day:

- "Do you live here?" (*No, we commute daily from Miami.*)
- "Do planes fly in here?" (*As a Cayman Airways jet is on final approach, and the sound of the engines is so loud I have to lean forward to hear the question ... but I*

already know the question, having heard it before!)

- "Are we getting lunch on this trip?"
- "How many reefs are we going to?"
- "Is the coral real or plastic?"
- "Is this a snorkeling trip?"
- "Do cruiseships come here?" (*Duh! You just got off one!*)
- "How deep is the sand?"
- "If you go deep enough, can you go all the way under the island?"
- "What holds the island in place? A chain?"
- "Does water go all the way around the island?"
- "How far is the ocean from the beach?"
- "What time does the 9:30 trip go out?"
- "I spit into my mask and it keeps flooding."
- "Are those flying fish?" (*"No, they're swimming birds,"* a straight-faced divemaster replied. After contemplating this for a moment, the lady asked, "Where do they nest?")

After answering a few questions, we're attaching the boat to a permanent mooring on a shallow reef. This one happens to be Cheeseburger Reef (Burger King is visible on the shoreline).

The briefing on how to snorkel and how to choose equipment that fits is being given by Michael Grundy, who, with his British accent, can get away with saying many things to tourists that I wouldn't *dream* of saying!

As he briefs on choosing a mask, he mentions that Vaseline provides a seal for men's facial hair—and asks out loud, "But ... I want to know *why* you have Vaseline on this trip, guys!" Howls of laughter ripple through this group of elderly travelers.

The people are finally splashing around happily in the water. You can hear occasional screams as fish come directly at them, looking for a handout of food. For added entertainment, one of the crew goes underwater on scuba to hand-feed the fish. As it is always the newest divemaster who gets this job, Michael's quirky sense of humor gets another chance. Unbeknownst to the new crew member, a large piece of bread has been stuffed between his dive gear and scuba tank. Seen from the snorkelers' perspective, it looks as if the diver is being devoured by yellowtail snappers and sergeant-majors. In fact, we've nicknamed them the "local piranhas". The divemaster down below thinks the fish are being unusually voracious today! As he's feeding the fish, the rest of the crew are up above, problem solving:

- "No, the mask doesn't cover your mouth."
- "Yes, the snorkel mouthpiece must be all the way in your mouth." (*And sealed by your lips!*)
- "Yes, the gear was cleaned between trips."
- "Yes, the fish are hungry!" (*As the tops of the guy's ears are bleeding under the assault of munching fish.*)
- A lady wants to trade her turquoise-colored fins for black ones, because "these keep fading on me!" (*She also had turquoise paint on her thigh that had rubbed off the boat bottom.*)
- "Yes, the water is salty."
- "The nose pocket of the mask does *not* go on your forehead—it covers your nose!"

And my all-time favorite ...

I looked to the boat platform and saw an elderly gentleman clutching the ladder. As I walked over to assist him, it crossed my mind that he could be having a heart attack, so I quickly went through the CPR steps in my mind. He slurred, "I lost my dentures!" I suppressed a laugh and asked him to board the boat so we could figure out what to do about his loss. Sting, a crew member, was great at breath-hold diving, so he went in search of the dentures. Within five minutes, he proudly surfaced, dentures in hand. The gentleman gave the divemaster a hundred-dollar cash tip, gargled a "thank you", and commented how his vacation had been saved because he still had two other islands to see ... so imagine our shock when he placed the dentures in his mouth, shifted them into place, then loudly proclaimed, "These aren't mine."

Moments later, the fish-feeding diver came up and asked "Did anybody lose a pair of dentures?" Those *were* his!

Another tooth story involved a cruiseship snorkeler who began hollering all of a sudden, "My tooth—my *gold* tooth—just popped out! My tooth!" The divemaster jumped in just in time to see the gold tooth spinning toward the bottom, only to be sucked up by a hungry yellowtail snapper.

After a couple of years of cruiseship questions, I asked another boat captain if he was getting any funny questions. The *KonTiki* was a rum punch/live band double-decked glass-bottom party boat. The captain said the most *common* question was "What deck is the glass bottom on?"

Years later, after hearing our cruiseship stories, Eric and Holly Lindauer, guests of ours, brought in a cruiseship captain's list of favorite questions.

- "Do these stairs go up or down?"
- "Which elevator do I take to get to the front of the ship?"
- "If the pictures aren't marked, how do we know which ones are ours?" (*Photos of the guests are taken at various events on the cruiseship and are for sale.*)
- "Do we get wet on the snorkeling trip?"
- And my favorite: "What do they do with the ice sculptures after they've melted?"

In the outer islands, a boat captain in Cayman Brac heard the funniest question, I thought. They had been going in and out the Brac channel, which is *very* small and close to shore. On about the fifth day of diving, the boat was headed out, and the captain overheard a lady who had turned around and seen the island asking another diver, "What island is that?"

A cute story from Little Cayman: after I dive, I grab a quick fresh-water rinse and change into a dry bathing suit. One reason not to stay in a wet suit is that on a windy day you get chilled staying wet—plus, if you stay in that suit, after a time you tend to get skin irritations, from salt water combined with sweat and heat. Well, a young woman on the boat had seen me drive out to the dive site. After the first dive and the first wet-suit change, I went upstairs to drive to the second site and she asked, "Does your bathing suit change colors when it gets wet?" Of course, we laughed, but you have to remember that nowadays there is nail polish that changes colors in the sun, so it's not *too* farfetched an idea that a suit might change colors! I may need to talk to the manufacturers ...

Another boat captain who had done many snorkeling trips told of a snorkeler who kept colliding with the boat and actually bumped his head several times as he drifted down beside the boat. As he boarded the boat, he had patches of blue color throughout his hair. The boat's bottom paint had rubbed off on him. The captain said he looked like a wind-up toy in a bathtub. I can *see* it happening. I guess that means I did one too many cruiseship snorkeling trips myself!

After weeks on end of these cruiseship trips and questions, a lot of divemasters go for a dive on their day off, and it's a bit different from the dives during the week: deep. There are now written rules about depth limits in our Cayman Islands Water Sports Operators Manual. This manual was created so that all the operators have the same diving rules and etiquette, along with emergency procedures and safety rules. I was never interested in "the Deep", but a friend who is told me this story.[1] Two divemasters had gone for a dive, dropping off the wall and descending to 180 feet. All of a sudden Jim[2] heard a popping noise. He calmly reached back to check that all his regulator hoses were okay. Everything seemed all right, so they continued down. At about two hundred feet, the same persistent popping noise occurred, right by his ears, so he took off his gear and spun it around to visually check for any problems. None. He looked over at his buddy, who seemed unperturbed by anything. A little later, a little deeper, the advent of a little nitrogen narcosis made Jim feel less and less concerned about any unusual noises. At the deepest part of the dive, around 220 feet, he said he finally figured out what the popping noise was: the water pressure had imploded the Cheez Whiz can that was in the pocket of his buoyancy compensator. He used it to do the daily fish-feeding shows for the cruiseship passengers.

Hopefully, cruiseships will never be allowed in Little Cayman. In fact, over the years, a small but committed community has been able to avert those few that planned to come here, persuading the powers that be to change their route to Cayman Brac. Our island has no infrastructure, no taxis, nothing to offer masses of tourists. Over time, I have seen the island and the people who come here change a little, but it's still a really special place. A funny story: one of Little Cayman's main attractions is the Booby Pond. The Caribbean's largest concentration of Red-footed Boobies and Frigatebirds roost along the shore of this pond at night. Of course, with that many birds on a daily flight path to and from their nests, you can imagine what the pond water consists of ... in fact, when the pond partially dries up in response to seasonal changes, the mudflats smell exactly like rotten eggs. You could not *pay* me enough money to go in there. ... but two tourists were seen snorkeling in the pond. Yecch!

One of the Cayman Islands' primary tourist events is Pirates Week. Everyone loves costumes, right? On the big island, there are huge pirate ships and re-enactments of cannons firing, pirates walking the plank to plunge into the sea, etc. In Little Cayman, it began as a drive to the far end of the island; as the Cayman Brac boats would come to "take over" the island, they were bombarded with airborne coconuts and huge water balloons. It has now evolved into a colorful parade, with resorts and residents creating their rendition of history.

The parade of floats and trailers begins at Head O' Bay, and with shouts of "Aarrr, matey ..." the trucks make the two-mile journey to the Hungry Iguana parking lot. Judges are flown in from Grand Cayman to make sure that the awards for best float and best costume are bestowed, without bias, on the most deserving. Of course, a pirate's outfit is pretty easy: shred a T-shirt, put on an eyepatch and tie a scarf on your head, start cussing colorfully, and you're in the competition. However, the costumes have become more and more outlandish over the years. In one of the most recent parades, there were some extremely elaborate and expensive outfits from Seattle. The men work for some pirate committee back home and wear these costumes at fundraising events. I believe they were used to a more civilized event, because when the water balloons started bursting near them, they haughtily announced how much money their costumes were worth. Oh, well ... too fancy for Little Cayman.

That's one of the special things about Little Cayman. For a lot of the homeowners, their Cayman Island getaway is their second or third home, but they mix and blend in—there are not many prima donnas here. The funny thing about the parade, at least for now, is that there are more people IN the parade than there are along the roadsides watching.

In the Cayman Islands, the National Trust is concerned with conservation and preservation of our environment and Caymanian cultural heritage. It purchases land for conservation, preserves historic buildings and sites, and in general educates people about Cayman's natural resources and how to protect them. There are threatened and indigenous species of plants and animals that the Trust is trying to protect, and it helps make people more aware of what is precious in these islands. The Little Cayman committee of the National Trust was started by Gladys Howard, As president, she foresaw the need for a community and interpretive center near the village. When she discovered that no funds were available for that project, she wrote a cookbook, containing recipes from Pirates Point Resort, called *Cook'in Little Cayman*. All of the proceeds went toward making this interpretive center a reality. As time has gone on, other functions have raised money to purchase land around the Booby Pond, and the land adjacent to the road by the pond has been designated a Ramsar site and is thus protected by international convention.

Since I've mentioned Gladys Howard, I should point out that she is also the owner and manager of Pirates Point Resort, where I work and where I gathered these stories. Gladys had a successful catering business in Texas but had always wanted to own a resort. Her first dive instructor, Larry Smith, found the resort in Little Cayman for sale. It was really rustic, but with the same vision that resulted in the community center, she and her exceptional staff have created a unique and comfortable ten-room resort.

One of the National Trust fundraisers that is starting to draw a pretty good crowd is the Easter Auction. Each year, hundreds of items are donated to the National Trust, and Betty B., Gladys, Sue L., Brigitte, and other community homeowners and resort staff set up the items for the big day. Some items are sold by silent auction, and later in the evening, items are shown off "Vanna White" style, and the highest bidder goes home with some unique treasure. Items are varied—housewares, gifts, funky candles, handheld radios, handwoven silk robes, restaurant meals, resort stays, and lots of beautiful local art depicting island life. Every year, John Mulak has donated a spectacular carved island bird that draws some of the biggest bucks. Most people who buy the birds have left them in the display cases at the National Trust house for educational purposes. Some of the heavy hitters have an ongoing challenge to see who can donate the most ... or so it seems. You often hear comments like "It's for a good cause ... it's for the National Trust" as the value of the donations rises. All the people here donate time or talents toward saving the treasures of Little Cayman.

Some years ago, I was helping with the auction when I realized that a rare conch pearl was up next. I asked Pete[3] to bid for me, but to watch me for hand signals— a thumbs-up meant "keep raising the price" and a slash across the throat meant "let it go". It started out cheap, but Jeff S. was interested also. Oh no! I kept hesitantly raising my thumb, biting my lip and thinking "It's for a good cause ...". I nearly cried when I saw Jeff losing interest and no others joining in on the bidding. The final bid was around six hundred Cayman dollars, which translates into about eight hundred U.S. dollars—but hey, they're rare! The funny part: the next day, Jeff came by and we were talking about the auction and how much money was raised, and I mentioned the conch pearl. That's when he told me he had been bidding against *Pete*, but gave up after a while. He said, "I was trying to get it for you, Gay."

Eight hundred dollars later, I nearly fainted! The auction was another success.

2

Day-to-day Divemaster

The Cayman Islands have a great reputation—deservedly so. The underwater world is protected by a marine park, which allows no taking or collecting of sea life on scuba. It is also known for good weather conditions nearly year round, which create excellent visibility for divers.

Also, the Cayman Islands have a top-notch safety record—one of the best in the world. Our hats are off to the dive instructors, whose job it is to take people from a wide variety of backgrounds, with varying degrees of skill and amounts of time *out* of the water, and safely get them back *in* the water. It constantly amazes those of us who run boats how people who dive infrequently want the dive guide to think they are practically professionals. This, in itself, is where most of the problems occur. Dive instructors in the Caribbean rack up dives daily, so to have thousands of dives is the norm. The "average" diving tourist goes diving once a year, or once every other year, and collects ten to twenty dives a year. A *very* active non-professional diver might do up to fifty dives in a year. Yet ...

It's frustrating when dive instructors offer free hints or dive tips, only to get them thrown back by a tourist, with chest puffed out, saying something like "I've been diving since you were in diapers." Needless to say, this is one thing that leads to dive-instructor burnout.

If you went to a doctor for a diagnosis, wouldn't you listen? So why would a neophyte diver think he knows more than a dive professional?

Since this book was written for fun and as a guide to tourists ... my suggestion is to reap the benefits of the wealth of knowledge held by the professionals and people who live in an area unknown to you!

Following is a collection of first-day "funnies":

- Putting the dive gear on the scuba tank upside down.
- Wrapping the buoyancy compensator around the tank (for those of you who don't dive, the BC has a tank retaining band on the back).
- Jumping in the water without a weight belt, mask, fins, and just about every other necessary piece of equipment.
- In an attempt to go underwater, inflating, instead of deflating, the buoyancy compensator.
- Stuffing fire coral down a bathing suit, in an attempt to take home a souvenir (fire coral looks similar to cactus—you can imagine how painful *that* was).
- A guy trying to check in for diving on his brother's certification card. The picture was *not* him, but he had dived all over the world on it—we caught it. He was not certified to dive.
- A man complaining that his regulator hose was too short—the tank had fallen out of the retaining band and was dangling nearly to his knees.
- A guy asking if we sell "hand shoes"—he meant dive gloves.
- "Did you see all the garden eels?" *Yeah, especially the big green one!*
- A man asking if we do "gorilla" diving ... I assume he meant four or five dives a day?
- A lady trying to descend with the BC fully inflated—

she flipped over and tried frantically to kick under, but ended up looking like a novice synchronized swimmer.

- The reverse: a diver who failed to deflate his BC on ascent. As the air expanded, he flipped upside down to keep from ascending too quickly. He somehow ended up between the two weighted bars at fifteen feet, where the divers hang at the end of a dive to offgas nitrogen. As he kicked in this upside-down position, he kept going in circles. I nearly drowned laughing, as I observed the divers on the hang stop, their heads going back and forth, as if they were watching a tennis match underwater!

Most people come to the boat prepared to dive, with all their equipment in a bag. One day, though, we got a call to go to the Holiday Inn beach to pick up a family of four divers who had checked in and shown their certification cards to the dive shop the day before. We lowered the boat ladder to the beach, but could not believe our eyes: the only family of four coming toward the boat had *boxes* of newly purchased gear under their arms. I'm not kidding! The mask in a box, the fins in a box, the regulator in a box, the depth gauge in a box. In other words, one of us had to assemble all of the gear enroute to the dive site. If you want to look cool, this is *not* how it's done!

A lot of the dive shops do a courtesy pick-up at other hotels. I had done such a pick-up one morning from the Hyatt. I parked the bus, walked the guests into the dive shop to show their certification cards and had them sign a waiver. Since the dive shop faced a parking lot, I gave very detailed directions of how to go out, take a left, go through the lobby, past the pool to the beach, and the boat would be waiting for them there. The boat called by radio a few minutes later, asking if I had seen the Jones party. I said "yes" and that they were on their way. I received a second radio call from a frustrated boat captain, who informed me that everyone except the Jones party was ready to go. I decided to walk out and see if I could locate the two divers. Surprisingly, I found them on a couch in the lobby. When I asked what they were doing, they innocently replied, "We're waiting for the boat"— in the lobby! *Hello, anybody in there?*

One day at Pirates Point, a divemaster named Martha saw a woman scanning the bookshelves in search of the Cayman Islands bird book. Normal enough. But the lady was wearing a buoyancy jacket (used in scuba diving, in case you're a landlubber), which is *way* out of place in the library. Martha *had* to ask, "Are you diving today?" The lady's response, as if it were normal to wear dive gear around: "No, I'm just getting used to the equipment." Of course, to Martha or another dive instructor, the instant thought is "red flag"—maybe she shouldn't be going diving at all. (On her first dive, she was extremely well supervised!)

As a boat captain, you learn not only to observe but to listen ... just when I thought I had heard it all, I over-heard a conversation among divers.

One guy was SO excited. He and his buddy were stand-ing behind me, discussing the dive. "Did you see what *I* saw?" "No, what was it?" "It was either ... [pausing to think] a crab or a shark, I'm not sure which!" I wondered if it was safe to put these guys back in the water.

Then there was the couple spotted walking hand in hand along the waterfront, window-shopping in Grand Cayman ... wearing masks, fins, and snorkels. (We think it was a bet: someone bet they wouldn't do it—but they did!)

Cindy[4] worked at the front desk of a hotel. She was asked by a woman, "Do you sell vials or containers?" When Cindy asked, "Why?", the woman responded "To collect the lime-green, turquoise, and dark blue colors of the ocean."

Another funny thing you see as a boat captain is how people mark their gear. You're taught in dive classes to mark your equipment, just in case you're on a boat with other people who have the same gear. I have seen gear marked with different colors of electrical tape, nail polish in fancy designs, big "Wite-Out" initials, and various types of color coding. Some of the more memorable fin markings:

- TGIF on the fin pocket (*I know, you're thinking "Thank God It's Friday", as I did. But this stood for "Toes Go In First".*)
- "OZ lives" on back of fin.
- "Granny's fin" and "Granny's other fin". (*Actually, the grandmother, Sue Barnes, and her granddaughter Kirsten dive together and have the same fins. This is how they tell them apart.*)
- On the back of a pair of fins, "For a good time call Trudy" (on her left fin) and "949-6782" (on her right fin). (*By the way, the phone number is made up, so don't try to call Trudy!*)

On the surface interval, between dives, the conversation can become quite entertaining. We see all walks and stages of life, professionals and non-professionals. One day on the boat, we had three undertakers (no, they were *not* having a mortuary convention in the Caribbean!) and a guy who worked the carnivals. You never know who will be on the boat!

Usually the conversation is started by guests' questions, which get us off and rolling on past stories. One day we were going over underwater hand signals. These are standard signals that everyone must learn to become a certified scuba diver, but we were adding the signals for our area, the Caribbean.

- boat—cupped hands, to imitate boat hull
- eel—fingers pointed, open thumb out and back in toward fingers, to imitate the eel breathing
- lobster—two fingers on top of your head, mimicking antennae
- shark—the hand pointed like a fin, on top of head
- turtle—tight flipping of both hands, tucked in at chest level, to look like turtle flippers
- ray—arms extended out from sides, moving up and down, to imitate a ray's wings
- crab—both hands opening and closing like crab claws

At this point, a lady piped up with "That's not what *my* instructor told me 'crab' was!" (Now, you need to know that I am blond—mostly from sun—but this lady was really *a* blonde!) I knew this would not be good, but everyone was raptly attentive, waiting for the answer. So, I asked, "What did *your* instructor say 'crab' was?" She said, "My instructor said 'crab' was this" ... and proceeded to scratch her crotch area! Needless to say, everyone was speechless—you could see that she was the type to have believed him. After an awkward moment of silence, we decided to change the subject. *Everyone* was embarrassed for her—and she had no idea.

In Grand Cayman, fish feeding is a common thing—as opposed to Little Cayman, where it is not allowed at all. So I have to laugh when I remember the story of a new custom wetsuit. After you have lived here awhile and have spent a lot of time in the water, you never seem to be warm enough, so we are forever in search of the next thickest wetsuit. This particular suit had a "convenience" zipper installed in it, to allow the wearer to pee outside the suit. As he was using this custom feature, a large grouper was apparently checking out *his* feature and thought it resembled the sausages that get handed out as fish food. Imagine his surprise when the grouper decided to taste-test that "sausage". As the story goes ... the suit was for sale that afternoon.

Another story that's been passed around is this: There are two types of divers, (1) those who pee in their wetsuits and (2) those who lie about it. In Little Cayman we actually had a newly certified diver who would come up after the dive, stand by the stern platform, shake his leg a bit, and then sigh. When we asked what he was doing, his reply grossed everyone out: "Peeing in my wetsuit." This does *not* endear you to the dive staff or other guests.

It has been fun to see the changes in diving over the years. In the 1970s, the sport was undertaken mostly by men. Spearfishing and active interaction with the reef were common. In fact, in the old *Sea Hunt* movies, the hero was always getting tangled up, or in some danger, underwater. People never really thought about the impact of puffing up a puffer fish, holding turtles, grabbing a nurse shark's tail, flipping over conch, running their hands over soft corals, breaking off live coral to take a souvenir home, kicking coral with fins, squeezing sea cucumbers, or pulling on a lobster's antennae. All this behavior had an impact, however, and as the sport grew, divers in the '80s began to focus on conservation. Marine parks were established, and the macho aspect of the sport was being challenged as more and more women, and younger men with a different ethic, took up diving. In the '90s, the sport was all about travel and conservation education. By 2000, there was a definite change in attitude, and the "aggressive" diver is more the exception than the rule.

As boat captains and dive instructors, we observe divers on a day-to-day basis, which makes us extremely conscious of what we can do to help save the reef. We may not be able to stop development, change weather conditions, or improve septic systems, all of which have an impact on the reef, but we can educate divers—if they let us. That is one strength of Pirates Point Resort, where a lot of these stories come from—all the dive instructors are among the best. I have been told many times by guests that they learned something (no matter how many dives they had done), and the advice was given in an unobtrusive way. It's a constant process.

Three things I like about Little Cayman diving:

1. We ask people not to feed the fish because it alters their behavior. We have seen unbelievable fish behavior because it is all natural—feeding, mating, sleeping, interacting with divers, and on and on.

2. We do not wear gloves. People who wear gloves typi-
    cally touch and grope a lot more, unaware of the
    impact. If they were not wearing gloves, their hands
    would be slimy, as touching takes off the coral's
    protective coating. Imagine a boatload of people, all
    touching the reef, then multiply by ten other boats
    (possible at this time, from day boats to liveaboards—
    not even counting Cayman Brac day boats!) ... you get
    the picture. It is best to observe from a distance. I
    must also mention here the importance of not taking
    items below to "dig out" critters. Once a woman was
    getting ready to go in and I saw a spoon nestled
    between her not insignificant breasts. When I asked
    what for, she said it was for pulling things out to see
    them closer. Not on *our* boat! Little or no impact
    allows it to be here next year, and the next ... preven-
    tion is the key.

3. We practice buoyancy control. This is where Pirates
    Point stands out from other resorts (or so the guests
    keep telling me!). Obviously, we check certification
    cards, and then we take a bit of a history on each
    diver—number of dives, approximate date of last
    dive, how much weight was used on the dive, etc. We
    also ask about medical history. Since Little Cayman
    is still considered remote, it's best to be preventive.
    (However, a lot of people won't tell you; then if some-
    thing happens, they stammer ... "Well, this happened
    two years ago also.") Anyway, after the interview, off
    we go to dive. The first day we always like to see
    people in the water. Once we have observed them,
    they can either dive with a guide or buddy up and
    do their own dive. In a long-winded way, I'm describ-

ing how we do preventive maintenance of the reef. If someone is new or has not dived in a while, a dive instructor works with that person. If someone asks for a lot more weight than he needs, we suggest a buoyancy check and the first two dives with an instructor, so we can fine-tune the diver. The best way we can all help alleviate stress to the reef is to make sure divers have good buoyancy control. Also, the diver, being more comfortable, will see a lot more underwater. Good buoyancy control prevents accidents— it's a win/win situation. So why would people *want* to dive overweighted? Believe it or not, a lot of people say no one has ever told them they were wearing too much weight. So many things can be corrected by this simple skill—which has been given the name "Zen diving". Now you get the idea.

Another tip for dive travel in general is to trust the divemaster's choice of dive sites. Many tourists arrive with guidebook in hand, dive sites already preselected and starred in the book, and the idea that diving these sites will make or break their vacation. I remember one lady who pouted the whole drive back to the dock because we had been unable to dive Randy's Gazebo. Granted, it is a beautiful dive—just not in the conditions we found it in that week. That side of the island had nor'wester conditions for part of the week and ripping current or no visibility the rest of the time. (A nor'wester is a storm that typically comes in our winter months. Unlike our prevailing breeze, which comes from the south, this system comes from the northwest, bringing high winds and rough sea conditions.) There were better

dives that week, with great visibility and no current—
trust the professionals! The guidebooks have the dive
sites' names, but not the guides' knowledge of daily conditions.

Day to day, season to season, there may be certain
areas of the reef where mating behavior is going on, baby
drums have hatched, sponges are "smoking", or turtles are
feeding. I find that when nature has a show going on,
it's worth watching. We had a perfect example one August.
We had been consistently seeing four sharks coming into
the shallows, circling in search of lunch. We'd spent quite
a few dives observing their hunting behavior, but they
were not interested in or bothered by our presence. The
divemasters and guests had dived with the sharks, and
most of the group wanted to spend more time observing
their feeding behavior. However, two couples insisted on
going to Bloody Bay. They'd read about a beautiful section
of wall in Little Cayman and would not be deterred from
going there! So, as we moved to Bloody Bay, we called the
liveaboard dive boat to alert them to the action. About
an hour later, they watched the sharks repeatedly attacking and consuming a three-foot Southern ray. This is the
kind of thing you normally see only on Discovery
channel!

I think that people are just unaware of how special
things really can be—you can point out a seahorse or a
pipehorse, and inevitably the divers come onto the boat
and scream, "Did you see that barracuda?!"

As boat captains, we do try to fulfill dive requests.
One of the funniest lists of requests came from Winston.
I remember Winston for always being dreadfully seasick.
It could be flat calm, and I would see his backside as he

leaned over the rail to toss breakfast. We tried every known remedy for seasickness, to no avail. But at least he had a sense of humor! Some guests he had referred came down for a week of diving and handed me a list of dive-site requests ... written on an airline barf bag. Yep, that fits my memory of Winston!

Speaking of catering to the guests, Ann[5] had just become a divemaster at Pirates Point, and as I mentioned how we take care of the guests, she asked, "Where do we draw the line?" It seems that on the dive, a guy had started stroking her legs, getting extremely close to her crotch area. She stayed still, thinking he had mistakenly brushed against her as he adjusted his buoyancy. Nope—the second time it happened she turned around and saw him, but behind him was his wife—laughing hysterically. Apparently his wife and Ann had the exact same wetsuit, and the husband thought his wife was in front of him. Oops! That became a great joke about staying together with *your* buddy.

The dive shop is another place where you can observe a lot of funny events and comments. A dive couple in Grand Cayman, Sara J. and Gary, passed on this story. While Sara was working in the dive shop, an error was made on her banking account, and the bank sent a Caymanian woman with a paper for her to sign. As the bank clerk waited in the dive shop, Sara went to photo-copy some of the bank papers. The local woman looked around, admiring the pictures hanging on the dive shop wall. On the wall was a picture of a mermaid. When Sara got back to the dive shop, the Caymanian woman gazed at the picture with a twinkle in her eye and said, "So they really *do* exist?!" Sara, of course, responded questioningly, "You mean mermaids?" "Yes," said the local woman, "So they really do exist ... and she's black!" (The statue was originally a bronze mermaid, put into the ocean as a dive attraction. Over time underwater, the bronze had darkened to a near-black color.) Sara was shocked ("gobsmacked", in her own language) and tried not to grin, in shock that people might really believe in mermaids. They engaged in a conversation about diving, and it turned out that the Caymanian lady didn't even swim!

3

Cameras / Optical Illusions

*A*s I was collecting camera stories, most photographers cringed a bit and mentioned "tragic things happening to my camera" (Sue B.); "wild carnival rides" (Paul J.) of sea conditions when going to a site to photograph a particular sleeping shark; dry underwater housings leaking; batteries swelling ... a lot of the stories did not bring a pretty picture to my mind's eye. There were, however, some humorous ones ...

Cameras and photographs are a part of everyone's vacation. I can remember on every trip asking someone walking by to take a picture of my family or friends or husband and me in front of some landmark. The funny part is, after having developed the film, I haven't always been able to recognize where we were ...

In Grand Cayman, my friends Moke and Reid ran the underwater photo center for Don Foster's DIVE. They had quite a collection of beautiful underwater photos for sale, but the other part of their job was to develop and process film. One of their classics involved a gentleman who turned in a disposable camera to have the film processed into prints. After developing the film, it was anyone's guess as to what the subject was in twenty-three of the twenty-four pictures. These guys had seen everything, or so they thought. They soon began a contest to guess what was in the pictures. One picture was even posted on the counter. Any ideas? It turned out the picture was of a nose and mirrored sunglasses, meaning the guy had taken the photo with the disposable camera facing him instead of his subject. The last shot was a typical tourist subject, so we figured that at the last minute he must have figured out his mistake—however, not soon enough!

After he had come and gone from the photo center, "nose" jokes were common for some time: "This is my nose at the Turtle Farm", "This is my nose at Stingray City", "This is my nose on Cayman Airways" ... you get the idea.

On second thought, maybe he did it on purpose. Haven't you or any of your friends ever taken a teddy bear on vacation and photographed him at different locations? I know people who have ... but only secondhand! There have been newspaper articles about pink flamingoes stolen from yards and other "tokens" borrowed for posed photographs around the world, then safely returned.

Anyway ... pretty funny.

Speaking of cameras, Charlotte[6] used to work at a retail dive shop in Grand Cayman. One of their services was renting underwater video cameras; upon the camera's return, they would show the video on a big TV screen to promote further rentals.

Charlotte tells the story of being in the store when a couple returned their video camera. They were happily watching the big screen, when suddenly the film was no longer related to the underwater world. The camera had inadvertently been left on and was now showing the inside of their hotel room and their preparations for afternoon delight—on the big screen! "Okay, okay, we'll take the tape—just shut it off!" They could probably send this to Best Home Videos and win a prize.

Also in Grand Cayman, there is an annual Nikonos

underwater photo competition. Any of the divemasters on the island—from Sunset House, especially—can tell you some stories. The guests go below and shoot a roll of film, then surface to the boat and hand up the camera. The film is changed, and then they can go back down to shoot another roll. After having watched this up-and-down film change many times, P.J. decided to have some fun. P.J. was an English divemaster who always had a prank up his sleeve and a twinkle in his eye. He took an old, wasted Nikonos camera body down and pretended to shoot a roll of film. As guests observed, he sat in the sand, opened up the camera, and calmly traded the "exposed" roll of film for a new one. He said you could see them thinking "Why have we been going up and down to change film? Maybe we should try *his* way." Luckily, no one tried.

One day on the dive boat, I had a man with a *super* nice underwater camera and housing. Boy, did he look professional—until after the dive, when he asked *me* if I knew how to rewind the film!

Two stories stick in my mind from doing personal videos. A New Yorker wanted *everything* in his video—even if he didn't see it! So, there is a shot of him pointing, and an eagle ray goes by. He points again, and a shark is seen. Turtles, eels, angelfish—it was in the video.

For another video, I had asked Beth[7] what she wanted. She just asked me to film her diving underwater—simple. As we got to the sand bottom in about fifty feet of water, she pulled a big fake octopus out of her pocket. She put it over her head and jerked around, acting as though it was attacking her ... whatever!

Another videographer, Kelly, tells this story. She was

going to film one day and saw a diver standing on the sand with a strange look on his face. She gave him the "Are you okay?" hand signal and he responded by hand signal, "I'm okay." Since he wasn't damaging anything, Kelly swam on, in pursuit of more exciting divers. Later, he sought Kelly out to explain, "See, I can't pee while I'm swimming ... or even when I stop kicking. I have to have both feet firmly planted on the ground. It's like stage fright or something similar." WAY more than she wanted to know!

Here is another, in Kelly's own words. "One day I was getting a bit frantic at the end of my second dive, because I knew I needed at least a couple more minutes of footage to make my video sell well. But most of the divers were back on the boat, so I headed up to do my safety stop. To my incredible luck, a huge school of fish were in a frenzy just below the surface. I swam through them over and over for several minutes, just letting the camera roll. I was getting great footage because the fish were absolutely thick. I came up beaming happily, and the first thing the captain said was "What the HELL were you doing, swimming right under that guy puking his guts out over the side of the boat?!" Aargh!

These next two stories were donated by Jeff Anderson, who worked as an underwater photographer in Little Cayman.

"The wonderful thing about photography is the hidden emotion, detail, character, etc., that a good photograph bridges between the subject and audience. This is especially true in macro photography. Due to the magnification provided by the camera lenses, the resulting photographs often reveal detail not visible to the naked eye at the time the picture was taken. During one morning dive in search of small, elusive subjects, I noticed motion from a dark object in the white sand. It had the basic shape of a pipefish but was smaller than normal. Perhaps it was a juvenile. I didn't want to press my face too close to get a better look, only to have the fish swim away. So I began focusing the camera and taking shots. After a few frames, my buddy, a professional miniature-critter hunter, swam over to see what I was fussing over. As I pointed proudly to my minute discovery, I heard laughter from my buddy. It turned out my juvenile pipefish was nothing more than a piece of dark vegetation undulating across the sand with the surge!

"One Monday morning (yes, Mondays are still Mondays, even on an island) a customer walked into the photo shop and said her camera wasn't working right. My first step was to look through the viewfinder to see what, if any, information was being displayed on the LEDs. I noticed a lot of particles on the viewfinder glass, so I attempted to wipe them away. When I moved the camera, the particles moved too. I wasn't expecting that. What had happened was, the camera had flooded fully, complete with sandy sediment! No wonder it wasn't working right! Remember, underwater cameras work best when the water stays on the outside of the camera!"

Another dive-instructor friend, Paul Johnston, donated this story about "How to Be the Perfect Underwater Model".

"The first time a vacationing oceangoing diver watches fish being fed, it is a wonderful experience. During the week, the neophyte diver's confidence in ocean diving is being built up by the resort divemaster. As a treat for the underwater photographers in the group, the divemaster will offer to take the dive group to a special place to hand-feed the fish, stingrays, eels, or sharks.

"On the appointed day, the divemaster will tell the divers the exact procedure that is to be followed by the viewing divers and underwater photographers. The divers settle down on the bottom and then the divemaster begins to feed the creatures of the deep. Through experience, the divemaster knows the best food to use, the appropriate container in which to transport it, and the safe way to hold and release the food for the hungry sea critters. The divemaster puts on a good show with all the various slick feeding techniques he has mastered. All the divers are amazed and chatter about the experience on the boat ride back to the resort.

"You can bet, come the next morning, the new divers are going to feed the fish on their own. The male underwater photographer has color-coordinated his wife's or girlfriend's dive gear to look as good as possible. Pancakes, bread, sausage, and bacon are saved from the diver's breakfast and placed in scrounged containers for that day's photo session. Finally, the dive site is reached. Before the dive, the male underwater photographer instructs the diverette exactly what to do. He will go to the bottom and settle down, and then his lady will come down in her colorful dive gear, act cute, exhale her bubbles at the appropriate time, and feed the cuddly fish. Maybe she will even attempt to put a piece of food between her lips and let the little fishes gently kiss away the food. Has she got a big surprise coming!

"Well, the macho male has busied himself kicking up sand on the bottom, waiting for Ms. Diving Model to descend and do her thing. What these divers do not yet know about fish psychology is that these creatures have been conditioned to look aggressively for the food when it appears, and Ms. Diving Model is ringing the dinner bell. Here comes Ms. Diving Model! Macho Man is waiting with photographic gear posed. Uh oh! Ms. Diving Model needs to clear her ears. Focused on her ear clearing, she is unaware of the critters now starting to frantically circle her in ever smaller circles. Ears cleared, she reaches for the food in her BC pouch. Just as she gets her hand on the food container and gets its lid cracked open, the fish start attacking her hands, the pouch, biting her fingers, her hair, and her face. If her legs are not covered with a wetsuit, the fish are nibbling on her legs.

"In all the commotion, the bread or pancakes have turned into a milky liquid fog surrounding Ms. Diving Model. The fish are hitting her so hard around where she has the food container stored that she starts back-pedaling and shrieking into her regulator. She throws the container out in front of her and heads for the surface to escape the feeding frenzy. Macho Man will do one of two things. He will try to come to her rescue as best he can with arms filled with photography gear (you can imagine how effective he will be while being eaten alive by the fish) or he will start to laugh so hard at his lady companion's situation that his mask will fill up with water, so that he has to frantically swim for the surface, dropping his expensive photo gear to the bottom.

"Maybe the next day Macho Man thinks he can be a better model and lets the former Ms. Diving Model be Ms. Underwater Photographer. Same plan, roles reversed. Here comes Macho Man! So far, so good. He settles down and somehow maintains control of the food and begins to feed the fish. Now Macho Man is feeling cocky and wants a photo of himself that will electrify all of his buddies back home. Ms. Underwater Photographer will get one of the following photos to impress his beer-swilling buddies.

"Photo #1. A large green moray will come out from hiding and swim up his arm, into his BC, and stick its head partially out his BC collar and begin to sniff around Macho Man's ear. At this time Macho Man's eyes begin to shift to the left, and then to the right, and back again, and so on, like a Felix the Cat wall clock. Macho Man freezes in his tracks. Flash! Ms. Underwater Photographer has her picture.

"Photo #2. Here comes a giant grouper for Macho Man to feed. Having never fed a large grouper before, Macho Man has too tight a grip on the food and does not let go of it fast enough. Swoosh! The suction from the grouper inhaling the food sucks Macho Man's arm up to the elbow in the grouper's mouth. Now Macho Man is in the process of being eaten alive! Flash! Another winning photo by Ms. Underwater Photographer!

"Photo #3. Macho Man has overeaten at breakfast and has become seasick on the boat ride out. Undaunted, he still wants that once-in-a-lifetime photo of himself. Finally at the bottom, he goes through his performance. To be real cute, he will put food in his mouth and let the fish feed from there. In doing so, he swallows some salt water, which makes him gag. He upchucks his breakfast underwater, and the fish go wild. A hazy cloud and chunks of food swirl around his head. One of the fish takes a bite out of Macho Man's ear. Flash! Ms.

Underwater Photographer has taken the winning vacation photo!

"Yes, Mr. Macho Man will have some priceless vacation photos for his hometown buddies to see!"

One thing on an island that is synonymous with cameras and videos is island weddings. What a setting! At Pirates Point we have done many, and Gladys knows how to cater a beautiful event. We convert a thatch-roofed area on the beach into a wedding gazebo with local flowers, lace tablecloths, gourmet food, and champagne to toast the event. In this remote environment, it is simple, yet elegant. The vows are exchanged by the ocean as the sunset's colors change and fade away. Many beautiful pictures in albums and videos of toasts to past brides and grooms adorn the resort's lobby. After a special dinner, chosen by the wedding party, a three-tiered, ornately decorated cake is served for the finale. A video camera records these special moments so family back home can experience the island wedding.

Another option is a church wedding. For these events, a photographer can be arranged, and a pianist can accompany your walk down the aisle with "The Wedding March". Guess who the piano player is—ME! That was my life before diving!

Although these first two paragraphs sound like an ad for weddings at Pirates Point (please call 1-800-ISLANDWED—just kidding!), I wanted to mention funny things that I wish had been captured in photos or videos. One couple was getting married here with no attending bridesmaids or groomsmen. It was the third or fourth go-round for both. After the wedding, they proceeded to get drunk, listen to Willie Nelson in the bar by themselves, and then leave as an argument escalated. The next day, they were discovered to have slept in two different rooms. Valda, the resort's housekeeper, found the room next door to theirs, which had been ready for new arrivals, rumpled and disturbed. It looked as if the honeymoon was already over.

Then there was a beautiful wedding that could have graced the cover of *Bride's* magazine, except the bride was chewing gum. Now, maybe I'm just *too* observant, but I missed the wedding vows because the sound of gum being swished around in her mouth was a deterrent to me. I faced the wall and tried to focus on the next piano piece, trying not to let my chuckles sound out loud. When I glanced out at the audience, I observed people bending at the waist, disappearing behind pews, hands covering their mouths, to keep the laughter from escaping their lips. Of course, this made it harder for me—and the piano was in the front of the church, on a stage, behind the bride and groom! To go one step further, my mind started videotaping the wedding. Imagine ... at least she didn't pop bubbles.

There are spectacular church weddings. At one, every detail was perfect, a photographer's dream: silk ribbons on the pews, live plants in the foyer, gorgeous flower arrangements, beautiful dresses on the bride and attendants. It all went almost too smoothly—until the reception. As people were toasting the bride and groom, it began to get very warm. I thought it was because there were so many people in the room, it was the hottest month, and the air conditioning just couldn't keep the room cool. However, the next thing we realized was that the air conditioner had *died*, which was also indicated by the fact that water was trickling from the ceiling. Where do you think the drip was falling? On the wedding party's table! The table was pulled apart and buckets were put on the floor to catch the falling water. Their sense of humor survived, so this couple should be able to make it through whatever obstacles come their way.

4

Animal Stories

Most people lead very busy lives, and I loved reading a book once that called such people "human doings". The trend now seems to be to get back in touch with our feelings and slow down to enjoy the moment. I can't think of any better place than outdoors to feel that kind of peace. As you read this chapter on nature and animals, try to imagine actually seeing these things happening, or pretend you're videotaping the events and sharing them with someone. It's bound to bring a few laughs! Remember, it's all about "simple pleasures".

Ed and I live just six-tenths of a mile from where we work. One night, after finishing dinner, turning out lights, locking doors, and leaving the resort, I drove home, got out of the car, closed the door, got ready to walk inside, and heard a loud MEOW! I turned around to see Dash, one of the resort cats, lying on the roof of the car, claws dug into the rubber where roof met windshield, eyes as big as saucers, staring straight ahead. Obviously, he was as shocked as I was by his late-night ride.

The current resort cat, Mary Ann, has learned that at five o'clock her favorite snack, Cheez Curls, is served. As the guests come in for their happy hour drinks, they learn about Mary Ann's habit. Once she has had her treat, she shows her gratitude by drooling on whoever pets her next.

You have to admit, cats are pretty funny. They each have their own personalities, and every cat owner can attest to doing some pretty silly things to keep her cats happy.

Once when we were going on vacation, we had a fellow worker house-sit to care for Cali, our new calico kitten. He had come home, turned on the TV, fed the cat, and then decided to go to his own home to water his plants. When he came back, he could hear the stereo *blaring* as he came up the walkway to the house. He finally figured out that Cali had inadvertently (or not?) stepped on the remote control.

Cali is the most curious cat. She wants to know about everything and how it works. She knows every sound and smell in the house. As I was writing this book, I had some scented candles lit on my writing table. When I got my kitten, she was supposedly spayed; however, on this particular day she was in her "heat" cycle, which means she wanted to be as close to me as possible. She hopped up on the table, meowing and begging to be stroked. She rolled over and, before I could stop her, singed a bit of the long hair on her back. She immediately sat up, alert, sniffing around, trying to find out where that burnt smell was coming from. Of course, since it was behind her, she never quite found it ... but she sure did stalk it.

Birds are another popular island pet and can be quite entertaining. The Cayman parrots are no longer captured from the wild to be sold as pets. Since they were becoming endangered, the Cayman Islands passed a law to protect them. So many pet parrots are brought in— African greys, macaws, and so forth. Since my husband, Ed, likes birds, we sometimes get asked to babysit while the "parents" go away on trips. One of the funniest of these experiences was with a Yellow-naped Amazon Parrot. Ernie was the most talkative parrot I have *ever* seen. We finally ended up putting him in a different bedroom and covering him at night, just for a little peace and quiet. Ernie must have known he was a problem kid, because he would chatter incessantly, then out of nowhere he would yell "QUIET!" He would actually sit quiet and still for a few minutes, and then off he'd go again, *chatter chatter chatter ...* "QUIET!"

In Little Cayman, almost everyone has an iguana or two that have become tame. A guy called Glenn came and studied the iguanas here and said we probably had over two thousand. He tagged 250 with a system of color-coded beads on the back of their necks. He said the Little Cayman iguana is unusual because most iguanas don't have babies until they are five years old, but our iguana starts bearing young at two years of age. A lot of people can attest to the fact that our iguanas also have babies twice a year, whereas the norm is one batch a year. At Pirates Point Resort, we have a female iguana who was named Handbag by a divemaster, Alex, who had a rather sarcastic sense of humor. She has been there from the beginning of the resort and has created a safe home underneath what was once the generator shed but is now a workshop. She has survived everything we have, and more ... we have seen her chase off iguanas larger than herself in territorial battles ... and sometimes she didn't chase them off, as evidenced by the batches of baby iguanas she has every year. She is very tame and is hand-fed and stroked by my husband, Ed. Should I be jealous? So far, Ed chooses to come home to the condo instead of sleeping by the workshed with Handbag.

A quarter-mile from Pirates Point, a new residential area has been cut out that has already become known for quite a few *huge* "tame" iguanas. As people have started biking there, the iguanas have learned that a bicycle usually brings treats of bananas, grapes (which they love) or whatever the kitchens of Little Cayman donate to this adventure. One woman was surprised to be "attacked" by an iguana as she squatted with a yellow camera to take a picture. The camera must have resembled a banana! A guy related the story of a very large iguana stealing the *whole* plastic bag of food and dragging it off into the bush, leaving a trail of grapes. As the man bent to pick up grapes to regain control of the feeding, he turned to see eight iguanas chasing the grapes—and him!

Another story is of a day-long fight between a cat and an iguana—over a stale donut! Beggars can't be choosers. Now *that* is living on island time—sitting and observing ...

Sal and Andrea come every year to dive. One year, when they returned to Washington, DC, after a long day of travel, they left their dive gear to soak in the tub. They returned to find a little Cayman frog, looking questioningly at them from on top of the wetsuits. What to do? Can't FedEx him back; zoos don't want him. He was released in a nearby river ... so if someday you hear any funny news stories about frogs in Washington, DC—you know how it all started!

One of the most spectacular daily events in Little Cayman is the fights over food at the end of the day between the Red-footed Boobies and the Magnificent Frigatebirds. We have the largest concentration of these birds in the Caribbean. The boobies, which can dive into the water, are "bringing home the bacon" to their young, and the frigates, which cannot dive into the sea, are like pirates, attacking the boobies to make them drop the fish so they, the frigates, can have a free dinner.

Rod, a divemaster at Paradise Villas, had been finding random fish dropped on his path as he walked home. He thought this bizarre until he finally realized it was related to the aerial bird battle. The next week, as he was walking home, he was aware of the fighting birds. He suddenly heard a "plop" behind him, and turned to find a peacock flounder on the ground. I find this fascinating because peacock flounders are not only bottom-dwellers but extremely good at camouflage. So for a booby not only to see him but to dive in and get him is pretty impressive! Little Cayman is nature at its best.

Another friend, Nancy, who lived in this same area, tells of having a barbecue dinner gathering one evening. As they raised the lid on the barbecue to flip the meat, a fish head was donated from the heavens above. What are the odds?!

The preacher, Dan Shroy, and his family (Kathy, Caroline, and Matt) live right on the side of the pond where the birds come home to roost. They love to watch as their cats daily join in the game. Late in the day, the cats sit outside, watching, waiting for the occasional dropped fish. Then it becomes a race between cat, frigate, and booby as to who gets dinner.

One of their cat stories involved Sneakers, who was having some problems. The veterinarian had asked for a urine sample. The Shroys took the sample, which had blood in it, put ice around it, and put it in a padded envelope to be carried to the vet in Grand Cayman. Apparently the package was put in a pouch, but by the time it got to Grand Cayman the ice had melted, and there was concern that hazardous materials were aboard the plane. This occurred not long after 9/11, so you can imagine the scene it created on the tarmac at the international airport in Grand Cayman!

The Red-footed Boobies on the east end of Little Cayman and Brown Boobies of Cayman Brac have learned that if they follow the dive boats they get an easy lunch. As the boats cross to and from Little Cayman, flying fish are known to become airborne. The boobies follow the boats and either catch the flying fish in mid-air or dive into the water to retrieve them. Amazing.

Occasionally, we've had boobies flying close to the dive boat on our return home to the interior water, called South Hole Sound. We had all seen this particularly brave booby who kept trying to land on the boat railings, only to slip off. He then approached a dive boat from Little Cayman Beach Resort, a 48-room hotel, and landed on the divemaster's bald head. He slipped and slid, as he had on the boat railing, and finally, frustrated, took flight again. The best part was that someone was actually video-taping!

Another fascinating thing to watch is when the frigates are ready to mate. The male inflates a huge red pouch under his neck, as if to say "Look at me!" Jerry, the former manager of Little Cayman Beach Resort, tells of a lady coming into the hotel lobby, all excited, asking for his help. He asked what she needed, but she was dragging him outside, saying he had to help a bird. When he asked again what was wrong, she replied that the bird had swallowed a whole apple and needed help. Nope ... it needed a mate!

John and Marilyn Palmer, who built a house in Little

Cayman in 1986 and who have seen all kinds of birds over their years, related a funny tale. Marilyn said she heard an unfamiliar chirping one day and was so excited to think that a new bird had come to her yard. In Little Cayman, we do get some unusual sightings (pink flamingoes, pelicans, and other wintering birds that aren't normally resident here), especially after storms. She searched and searched for the "sighting"—until she finally realized it was the shower door! As it swung back and forth, it was making a chirping, birdlike noise.

Along with its spectacular birding, Little Cayman is, of course, best known for its wonderful diving. The island is essentially a mountaintop surrounded by open ocean and steep walls. The drop-off is six thousand feet deep! In the shallows, the water is shades of green and turquoise, gradually giving way to the deep blues as the water deepens. As divers, looking to the deep blues, we have seen some amazing sea creatures. Also, as a boat captain you can have unusual sightings of pilot whales, whale sharks, manta rays, dolphin, marlin, humpback whales, killer whales, tiger sharks—and who knows what else is out there that we *don't* see! I know that, since I'm into looking for *little* critters, I have sometimes not seen the shark or ray go by ...

We were lucky enough to see a marlin feeding on the surface one day. His blue and purple colors were spectacular as the sun bounced off him. As I shared this story with the local fishermen, they said they had rarely or never seen this before ... was I surprised. I thought it might be common for them.

One of the local fishermen, an electrical engineer, Mel, got on the radio one day to alert everyone to beware.

He had sighted a huge tiger shark in an area where people swim ... of course, half of us wanted to head out in skiffs to *see* the shark.

That reminds me of when I lived in Texas, and they would warn of a hurricane and huge wave conditions. Everyone would be evacuating the beach, while the surfers were piling their boards on their cars, heading *toward* the foaming ocean.

Martha, who works with me, shares a story from Florida. She was returning to the dive boat with some students and observed everyone bailing off the boat. Since Martha is a trained professional, she immediately started thinking of scenarios that would cause *everyone* to leave the boat quickly: fire, boat sinking, etc. As she surfaced, she asked the captain, "Is everything okay?" He pointed and said "Whale shark!" Martha got her students safely on board, out of scuba gear, and asked them if they would like to snorkel over and see the "once in a life-time" whale shark. As they responded with "No, we'll wait here," Martha was already into her snorkeling gear and gone—see ya! Of course the hope of seeing any of these special creatures is why divers go in, dive after dive, week after week ... what's next?

John, for years the Marine Parks enforcement officer in Little Cayman, had a special experience when he was a divemaster at Southern Cross Club. He was guiding some divers along the wall when, all of a sudden, out of the "blues", a sailfish came in and fed on some smaller fish on the wall, spun, and shot back out into the deep water. Chance of a lifetime ... and if he had blinked, he would have missed it!

On some dives, we wish we had a video camera, as

nature plays with us. Since the mid-1980s, I yearly dove a group from Florida. We called them the Huff group because of Jim and Debbie Huff, who always put the group together—Roger, Dave, Phil, Candy, Don ... One year in Little Cayman, Jim had found an octopus during the day and was trying to share his sighting with the group. He had the group's attention, took out his small dive light to point at the octopus ... and the octopus reached out, wrapped its tentacles around the dive light, and pulled it back into its lair. Jim never got the light back. Can't you see the mama octopus explaining to her baby about "tourists"?

In the Cayman Islands, manta rays are extremely uncommon, and my memory was that sightings seemed to be in migratory months. However, in Little Cayman we were blessed with a six-foot manta ray that stayed around for almost four years! In the beginning, there were occasional sightings ... as time went on, they became consistent, especially on night dives. She was called Molly, and toward the end of her sojourn here, she had become so well known that the Cayman Islands printed and distributed rules of how to dive with Molly and not harm her. She had become an attraction. In the earlier years, we had her to ourselves, and on night dives, she would find us! We would swim out to a mini-wall with a sand bottom, and as soon as we saw her, we would make a circle and point our lights toward the center. Molly would do barrel rolls, over and over, backwards, feeding on whatever the dive lights attracted—mouth wide open! You could see all the way through her. The circle was lit up like a stage, and she was in the spotlight. Incredible sight.

When the nor'westers came in the winter, we would lose sight of her for a while. We would not be doing as many night dives, and due to the weather, we would be diving the south side of the islands. Amazingly enough, however, Molly moved to the south side just as we did, and would surface just outside a channel called "the flats" (a shallow fisherman's cut in the fringe reef). During tidal changes, these natural cuts in the reef provided her with an alternative food source for winter. By summertime, we would be back up north for our nightly manta show, starring Molly.

In the early 1990s, we had a trio of wild dolphin that we were lucky enough to dive with many times. As we were driving the boat to a dive site, they would cavort and jump in front of the bow. I learned over time to just hook the boat up to the closest mooring, call it "Dolphin Alley" or whatever, and get in the water as soon as possible. In fact, it became so consistent that as soon as I saw the dolphin, we would get the people ready, so we would lose no time getting in the water, once the boat was secured.

One of my fondest memories is sitting in the sand with my group of divers, watching the three wild dolphin show off for us. They would dive down, bump their noses in the sand, flip over, race to the surface, twist and freefall back down, and then sometimes just lie still on the bottom for a while. Does the description accurately portray an underwater dolphin ballet?

Another year, there was a lone dolphin who became known as Spot because of his body markings. The word is that young male dolphins leave a pod for a while to "sow their oats". Later, they return to a pod and possibly take over from an aging male dolphin as the leader. Spot stayed between Little Cayman and Cayman Brac for about two years. At first, I was never lucky enough to see him. The other dive instructors who worked with me at Pirates Point would come home, beaming, with yet another Spot story. Talk about frustrating! Finally, after hearing "Spot this ... Spot that ... and then he swam around us ..." for about two weeks, I finally had *my* day.

Jerry[8] and I were out for the day's dives. I was guiding the certified divers, and Jerry had a student who was doing his first open-water training dive. In other words, the student had done pool and class work back home and today was doing the pool skills in the ocean for the first time. What a cool experience in itself! So, off I went ... as I was coming back to the boat, I glanced up to see Jerry and his student making their way down the stationary mooring line where the boat was secured. My mind wasn't registering that Jerry now had *two* students ... the dolphin was coming down the line with them! Imagine, this is your first dive EVER, and a dolphin is descending with you and your dive instructor! Just hang up your fins—it doesn't get much better than that!

My group decided to play with Spot. I sat off to the side, observing what he liked and didn't like, hoping to get insight for the best experience, After about fifteen minutes, he swam over just above me, dove down to me, turned around, put his flukes in the sand, and leaned back against me, head almost lying on my shoulder! Luckily, a guy videotaped it, because no one would have believed me. In fact, in the video, you can see my look of "I *hope* you're getting this on video!" As I watched the video later, I saw Jerry and his student swimming by ...

Jerry shaking his head, like he couldn't believe the dolphin was doing what he was doing with me. I couldn't believe it either. In fact, I have replayed that mental tape in my head over and over. Needless to say, this explains why I continue to dive, and why people *do* dive. There is a lot of ocean out there, and who knows what nature will provide for our next treat?

Sometimes nature provides a variation on the norm. In Little Cayman, our average annual rainfall is ten to twelve inches. One October, we had incessant rain—days and days of it. There was so much excess water that the various ponds flooded their banks. Whistling ducks and tarpon were swimming randomly down what yesterday was the main road. There was a tarpon round-up held to safely net the fish and return them to their island pond. The whistling ducks enjoyed a *huge* pond for a couple of days. As the water receded and they returned to their original ponds, you could see the confused look on their faces. Some were seen waddling down the dry road with a look that seemed to say, "Yesterday I was swimming here! What happened?"

Often after tropical storms, as we dive the familiar sites, it is amazing to see the dramatic changes in the underwater sand topography. Even the fish seem lost. I have seen sand-dwelling fish—tilefish, jawfish—up on the reef, looking for their familiar holes. They can be seen rebuilding their underwater holes by dragging rocks and sand, mouthful by mouthful, to the surface of the hole and spitting it outside their home. Many of the reef fish, likewise, are thrown off course and are frantically crossing miles and miles of sand in search of the coral head where they used to have a "condo".

As I am interested in fish behavior and the small critters, I'm always looking for the next cool thing to show our guests. It's an underwater adventure—and nature provides a great show. We were diving on the dramatic Bloody Bay drop-off when I noticed two squid. I alerted the group to hang out and observe, because the squid behavior was different from normal. What luck! The squid were laying eggs under a sponge! At the beginning, the squid were a happy, blue-purple color, and then, as we watched they suddenly changed to a brown and beige coloration that ran down the length of their bodies. The male would flare his tentacles, as if guarding, while the female kept laying repeatedly under the same sponge. I kept edging closer. At that time, I had long blond bangs that flowed around in the water. The female squid must have thought my hair looked like the tentacles of another squid, and she could probably also see her reflection in my mask. She felt around my bangs for a couple of minutes and then must have somehow communicated to the male that it was time to go, because they inked in unison, then propelled themselves quickly out of our sight. I looked at the others with my mouth hanging open (well, almost ... kinda hard to do on scuba!), and the guests were as surprised as I was!

Another "close encounter" happened to Martha, one of the five dive instructors at Pirates Point. Coco and Martha had taken the boat out and, due to weather, were on the south wall dive sites. Martha was getting a guest back in the water who needed a bit of extra time and attention. Later on, they caught up to the group on the wall, just in time to see Coco pointing out a huge hawksbill turtle. It was actually sitting on the coral (something we ask our divers *not* to do. What an example!). The turtle slowly started to swim, so Martha did a quick, tight flapping of her hands by her shoulders, imitating turtle flippers. Lo and behold, the turtle came closer! Cool. What a great experience for Susan,[9] to get back into diving and have a turtle come so close. What a view! Martha did a couple more flaps of her arms, and the turtle kept coming ... until WHACK! It must have seen its reflection in the mask lens and was protecting territory, but he hit Martha's mask face plate so hard it split the mask and put a gash on her forehead. Of course, being the professional divemaster she is, she took a look down the wall, grimacing where the guest couldn't see the surprise in her face, then continued with the dive. No more turtle attacks occurred. They finally surfaced, and as Martha took off her mask and the pressure was released, the blood flowed from her forehead. Coco and Martha have a great relationship and are always teasing each other, so Coco's first comment when she saw the blood was "What did ya do? Run into a coral head?" Luckily, a few of the guests could vouch for Martha's story. It's funny, because Martha says she has done this turtle-flipper action "thousands of times" and never had this happen. I must say, too, that in all of our divemasters' dives, collectively (can you *imagine* how many dives that is?), no one had seen this before.

The second half of this story is that Martha went to our island's small clinic to get a tetanus shot from Nurse Mary. Of course, Martha tried to think of a way to fudge the story a bit. (You know how quickly stories get around ... newspaper headlines!) Finally, she told the truth, and she said she could see Mary's shoulders shaking as she was getting the shot ready, trying to control her laughter.

Martha finally told her to go ahead and laugh, just not to spread the story.

5

Planes, Barges, and Automobiles
(and other transport)

It's inevitable that people living on a remote island like Little Cayman would have stories involving planes. Before I moved here, my best friend from high school, Janet, was moving to Antigua for a year with the Peace Corps. As her small plane was taxiing down the runway, she glanced out the window to see all her luggage on the tarmac! This was *her* start to island life. She called to warn me, and since it was my first trip on an island-hopping plane, I was very alert anyway.

The year was 1980, and I had just become heavily involved in diving, so my eye was on my dive bag. The gear handlers put my yellow bag in the luggage compartment, then took it off. As I was about to go talk to someone, the handlers put the bag on the other side of the plane. My immediate thought was "They must be balancing the weight." After ten more minutes of shifting luggage, we were ready to go, and my luggage was in place. As the plane started taxiing, I let out a big sigh, from relief and a little bit of nerves. This traveling takes a lot out of you. The next thing I noticed, the plane was turning and heading back to the terminal. The pilot must have sensed our questioning looks, because he turned around and said, "I guess we better fuel up before doing the crossing!" *Duh!* You should have seen our faces! The baggage balancing must have distracted them from fueling!

On to Little Cayman ... to anyone interested in coming here, you should know that there is *no* boat ferry serving our island. We are eighty miles from Grand

Cayman and about ten miles from Cayman Brac. The sea conditions between islands can even keep the liveaboard dive boat in Grand Cayman, so a ferry service would be inconsistent and weather-dependent.

The plane is the only way in here. Island Air, the inter-island service, has a couple of planes. The main one is a nineteen-seat Twin Otter with huge viewing windows that allow you to appreciate the scenery as you fly in over the turquoise water and land on a grass runway. It is always fun to watch people's expressions as they deplane. Some look as if they want to kiss the ground! In the earlier years, with a much smaller plane coming in, there were times that the plane could not land because the grass had grown so high. At that time, the 3,000-foot grass runway was trimmed by Jack, who would walk its length, swinging a machete to trim the tall weeds. Nowadays there is a riding mower—progress!

In the event the "big" plane is fully booked, there is a backup plane that can be chartered. Sometimes the weather or sea conditions do not allow our tug-and-barge service to bring us supplies on time, so we charter the plane to bring in people, food, whatever is needed to make it all work.

Gladys had just hired a new chef from California, only to find out that the flights were all sold out. Since timing is crucial and we operate with a small staff, we were anxious to have Gregg come on in and put on an apron. At the same time, because the barge was not able to come in, we needed some fresh produce to tide us over. All the food at Pirates Point Resort—fruit, produce, homemade breads and desserts— is fresh daily. The use of canned items is not an option. So, Gladys chartered the plane and told Gregg where and when to meet his "ride" to Little Cayman. I will never forget his face ... imagine, you have never been to this remote island; you have traveled *all* day from California, after having talked to the resort owner only by phone; you land on a grass airstrip with a case of pineapples in your lap and cases of fresh produce packed tightly around your seat. Welcome to your new job in paradise! I wish I could have heard his first thoughts.

I can also relate, though, because at one point Ed and I had a small Piper Cherokee four-seat plane. It was fun to pop over to Grand Cayman for dinner and a movie, then fly back in time for work the next day. However, with each successive flight, we felt more and more as if we needed a freighting company name on the side of the plane. We would get to the plane, already loaded with supplies, to find a cart full of items that had been dropped off to come to Little Cayman with us! On one of our last flights with our plane, I re-enacted Gregg's trip, but instead of pineapples in my lap, I held a *huge* filter for the 40,000-gallon swimming pool at the resort. It totally blocked my view of the landing! My favorite part is seeing the varying shades of the ocean as the color goes from deep blue to turquoise to light green in the shallows.

The owner of another private plane, Larry B., was a developer who built some of the first condominiums and houses in Little Cayman, in the early 1990s. He would go to Grand Cayman or Cayman Brac to pick up supplies as needed to keep the building project moving forward. Often he would be flying in after the "thirty minutes after sunset" rule, which is the latest a light plane can land in Little Cayman, since there are no runway lights. Larry had flown in so many times at later hours that he knew the lights of the "village" like the back of his hand. Imagine his surprise one night, as he lined up with the now-familiar lights, to find the lights moving! He circled, because the lights were all of a sudden *un*familiar—and they kept moving. He finally realized what it was, and came on in for a safe landing, chuckling to himself. It turned out to be some local people, out with flashlights, looking to catch some land crabs for dinner.

In emergencies, the trucks on the island are called out to line the grass runway so that the airline pilots can find their way in after the sun goes down. Luckily, this procedure hasn't had to be used very often—but it does work!

Most of our repeat customers and friends call before they come, knowing how difficult it is to get things here, and ask if they can bring us anything. Bill was coming our way in a private plane with Dickie and had asked for our needs. They arrived packed to the gills—and Bill, not being the pilot, had bicycle tires around his neck and a grin on his face. The joys of owning a small plane ... and going to a small island!

Since Pirates Point is known for its food, we have had many people fly in just to experience Little Cayman and a gourmet meal beside the sea. One such experience sticks in my mind. We picked up six people for a day spent hiking, observing nature, sharing a great lunch and companionship. End of story. About a month later, we received six linen napkins in the mail, along with a note saying how comfortable they had felt in our "homey" atmosphere and explaining that they had inadvertently stuck the napkins in their pockets as they were visiting with our guests!

Earlier, I said the plane was the only way in here. It is ... on a daily basis. In the past, before Island Air started the service, a different plane served Little Cayman, but not a daily service like nowadays. The plane frequently had problems and broke down, so Frankie B. would be hired to take people to and from Cayman Brac in his boat, *Sea Wolf*. One of my memories is of Frankie leaving Southern Cross Club's dock early one morning with guests and luggage from each resort *piled* on. A moment before, they had all been standing on the dock, eyeing each other and the luggage, wondering how in the *world* all of them were going to fit! Frankie strategically balanced people and luggage until there was no deck space left, then told the people not to move "until we get to Cayman Brac!" How *could* they? Luckily, it was a flat calm sea, but as the people left the dock, their expressions indicated that they did not appreciate the conditions. You could almost see *Titanic* playing in their minds. I could imagine someone yelling "Turtle on this side of the boat!"

Lost Baggage

Inevitably, when transporting baggage to a small island by air, some days it just doesn't all work out. Of course, the tourist must learn to streamline the packing. We had a visitor who had *fifteen* pairs of shoes in her room. That was just the shoes! Now, imagine her bags not making it the first day. Is it worth getting upset over clothing? To some people, it might be, but a word of advice is to pack according to the island you are going to ... big island, big bags; small island, small needs, small bags.

A couple arrived on the last flight of the day with NO bags. I loaned the lady a dress for dinner, T-shirts were purchased, and we made them as comfortable as possible. We even sell toothpaste and toothbrushes ... just in case. We assured them that the airlines are great at tracking lost bags and that the bags would almost surely be here the next day. The next day, we made multiple calls back and forth to the airlines, hoping at least to hear that the bags had been found. No luck. Day 2 featured the same desperate phone calls, and at some point, I realized that the airline attendant was as frustrated as we were—but neither of us gave up hope.

The couple by now was dressed to look like us—nice outfit! Day 3, we had all but given up, when the attendant called us, excited that she had found the bags and they were enroute as we spoke! Her relief could be heard on the phone. I heard the plane arrive, so I drove quickly down to collect the lost bags. They looked like their description, but no name tags were attached ... hmmm. After dropping the bags at the couple's room, I returned to the clubhouse/office for the next challenge. All of a sudden, I glanced up to see the couple, faces long and drawn, staring down at me. "What's wrong?" I asked with concern. "It's not *our* bag." That knocked the wind out of my sails, as they say. Then—not to sound ignorant, because I was sure they knew their bag and what they had packed—I had to ask, "How can you tell?" Their deadpan response was ... "The bag is filled with sweaters, mittens, and ski caps." If I hadn't seen their faces, I would have laughed out loud ... however, it was no laughing moment. The next phone call was truly awkward—the attendant for the airline had worked so hard to find the bag. When I told her it was the wrong bag, I could hear the restraint in her voice: "It *has* to be the right bag ...".

When I described the contents of the bag, and she knew we were calling from a Caribbean destination, the only response was ... silence.

My other favorite luggage story happened to a guy named Tex[10] (he actually *was* from Texas!). Tex came into town one day with several large suitcases and an excess-baggage fee that was bigger and better than anybody traveling before him. We stuffed the luggage into the van, drove him to his room, then filled his porch space completely with bags. Moments later, he was at the office with a problem. Surely, he had not forgotten a bag! No, one of the bags was not his. He had actually picked the bags out of the luggage carrier at the airport, paid extra money for them, and dragged them to the resort and up onto his porch. I don't know what y'all call that, but in Texas (where I'm from), he would be called an "Aggie". (An Aggie is someone who attends Texas A & M University in Bryan. A & M stands for Agriculture and Mechanics, so the kidding comes about because the "guys" are typically farmers and not too sophisticated.)

The saddest luggage tale happened not in coming here but to a guest returning home. Jerry, from California, had returned home after a full day of travel, but found out his luggage did not make the same trip. A missing bag has probably happened to each of us at some point in our travels. The airline assured Jerry that the bag would be brought out to his house when it was found. On Monday, Jerry's wife answered a knock on the door and found an airline employee, delivering the lost bags. She was immediately suspicious, however, when the outstretched hand held not a familiar piece of luggage but a large black garbage bag. Opening the garbage bag, she found Jerry's dive bag—in hundreds of pieces! Somehow his bag and its contents had gotten shredded on a misbehaving conveyor belt. He mentioned that his dive knife, which is an extremely sturdy item, was in ten different pieces. It seemed the garbage bag was the appropriate choice, because *all* of his gear was garbage now.

Luggage is not the only thing that gets delayed. FedEx, even to Little Cayman, is known for its promptness. Of course, "next day" is not an option, but two or three days seems normal. I believe, however, that somewhere in Grand Cayman there is a shelf where random items get placed for a while. Anyway ... one of our repeat customers had FedExed some items on February 21st, and the items reached Grand Cayman the following day. He arrived on March 2nd, but no FedEx had come ... it arrived March 4th. In case you need to reread the time log—the items got to Grand Cayman on February 22nd. Where were they for ten days? The Bermuda triangle/the Cayman mail triangle. The most frustrating part is the amount of time and the number of phone calls wasted on tracking down the missing item. At least this one showed up!

Sometimes mail delays can be caused by plane problems. On a rare rainy, dreary day in Grand Cayman, one of the big jets was coming in but had misjudged the landing and had problems with the reverse thrusters. The plane couldn't stop by the end of the runway, and its front half went into the sound. The sound is a shallow body of water inside the fringe reef. Since it *is* shallow, there was no threat of the plane's sinking; however, boats were needed to return the passengers and crew to shore. Of course, the island jokes followed:

We offer a complete fly/drive package.
Save time to the dive sites—fly our airline!
Fly-and-drive special ... call 1-800-SPLASH.

I heard they even made T-shirts ... use your imagination, and I bet you could come up with a few.

"How do you get your supplies in?" A common question, and the answer is: however you can! There is a tug-and-barge system that brings in wholesale items—beer, toilet paper, sodas, dry goods, produce, and other big-item needs—weekly. In the earlier years, it was not a weekly service, and once the resort experienced a period of no barge for three weeks. So ... at the resort, we try to keep enough back stock to last at least two weeks. Talk about being self-sufficient! Imagine rationing toilet paper ... just kidding. Nowadays, the grocery store is pretty well stocked with items. However, if *we* haven't seen a barge, due to weather, then neither has Little Cayman's one and only grocery/all-purpose store, about the size of a 7-Eleven.

Even in Grand Cayman, there are times when, because of weather, the big container ships cannot offload their supplies, so the goods on store shelves become a bit scarce. One day, when I was working in Grand Cayman, we were picking up lunch for the dive-boat crew. We hit the drive-thru at Burger King for a quick turnaround; however, they were out of burgers, out of this, out of that. BK is right on the ocean, where you could see the waves splashing on their parking lot—clearly the ships were not going to be delivering burger patties that day! You would never hear that at Burger King in the States: "Sorry, we're out of burgers today."

Back on Little Cayman, in earlier years, the barge

would tie up to the dock, and a representative from each resort would be there, ready to manually offload the containers—with "workin' on a chain gang" playing in our minds. Box after box, case after case. Luckily, at that time each of the three resorts had only ten rooms. Needless to say, not all of the items would make the transfer to the dock. A hastily tossed box sometimes fell into the sea, to be scooped out at a later time—a freebie to whoever wanted to go get it. As the island has grown, now the containers are driven to the top of the "hill". (Little Cayman is actually a flat island. The dock is lower than where they drop off the containers, so "hill" is a term used loosely.)

Containers coming from the U.S. are locked until the customs agent, Bruce or Larry, can assess, by invoices, a twenty percent duty on their value. The resort gets a U.S. container once a year, containing trucks, bicycles, hammocks, floor fans, new air conditioners, building supplies, box springs, and mattresses—whatever big items we need for the year. Sometimes we're so desperate for the supplies, we have actually taken our dive boat and docked up against the barge to get needed items. The barge company has a permanent mooring on the south side of the island, where the barge can tie up and wait for bad weather to pass. One March, the barge was being towed to the calmer side, but not before the seas pitched one, two, *three* containers into the sea. The first container slipping overboard unbalanced the load enough to cause the others to follow it. Once the containers hit the ocean, they split open, dumping the contents onto a fifty-foot-deep sand bottom. The concrete blocks that were meant for a new Little Cayman home instead became dwellings for juvenile reef fish. The funniest item was the cans of Coors Light, floating in their six-packs, free for the grabbing. The "coconut telegraph" got the word out, and within the hour, many boats had shown up to collect cheap happy hour beer. The other Sister Island, Cayman Brac, which is usually (depending on sea conditions) about a forty-minute boat trip away, even had representatives collecting floating "debris".

I've always sympathized with the crew of the barge. Have you ever been on a boat in rough seas? Now imagine being on a barge, pulled by a tug, yet pushed around by the sea conditions. On the rougher days, we have watched from the beach as the barge plowed into a wave, sending sheets of ocean spray high into the air, which then drops onto the barge deck. At times, the tug nearly disappears from view as it dips deep into the trough between waves. Now ... do this for hours on end, day after day. The rollercoaster ride at the theme park becomes child's play. Even though it is a weekly service nowadays, the weather doesn't always cooperate, and many times the crew spend their holiday at sea. I do remember one really bad nor'wester when the barge was attached to the south mooring, waiting for a break in the weather. I was watching from the Hungry Iguana restaurant, and as it was nearing Christmas, I was feeling kind of sad for the crew. But they had the spirit of Christmas on board. They had strung bright-colored Christmas lights all over the tug and barge. They lit up the dark night—no "Bah, humbug!" in this group!

Trucks and cars take a beating in the salt and sun of the Caribbean. Even if you Ziebart them (a treatment to coat the body and bed of vehicles to help them last longer), it doesn't take long for a truck to look like the Beverly Hillbillies' jalopy. Trucks eventually get their beds rebuilt in wood or get left at the dump to become public "parts" trucks. Once at the dump, the parts are fair game. The engine can be worked on and go on forever, but you would be sitting where? On many island trucks, the engines run great, but when you get in the truck, you have to pick the rusted door up off the ground and pull it into place—from *inside* the cab! Imagine driving along, being able to see the sky above you—or the road under the vehicle—as the truck body erodes away.

In the earlier years, our fuel for the dive boat was brought to us by a fuel truck. At one point, they were waiting for a brake part, so we were unsure whether we would need to collect the diesel in 55-gallon drums or if it would come to us. Imagine our surprise to see the fuel truck coming, but followed closely by another truck. The rear truck was "braking" the fuel truck down the small hill to the dock. Hey, we were laughing, but mission complete.

I remember seeing a Jamaican at a stop sign in Grand Cayman once. As the car was idling there, steam was continuously billowing from under the hood, pouring over the top, and blocking the view of the driver. I should say, *we* couldn't see the driver for the steam—but could *he* see to drive?

In Little Cayman there isn't a lot of traffic, but after a very close call in which one vehicle had to go into the bush to stop, the driver was asked why he was going so fast. The classic Caribbean reply was "I got no brakes."

The chief of police once said that traffic had gotten so bad in Grand Cayman that he wished they'd pass a law allowing you to bring a new car on island only after you retired one off the road. Neil Williams, the police officer in Little Cayman, says there are around 150 cars here now! I remember the story of the first two cars on the island having a head-on collision. Neil also says there are about 125 people living here full time, plus condo owners and homeowners who come for short or extended stays. Some homeowners come for six months at a time. Neil does a great job of keeping law and order in a small community, but he strikes a balance so that Little Cayman still has a nice ambience.

Sometimes, rusty or not, a truck is beyond your means, so bicycling is next best. In Little Cayman, there is constant bike swapping going on ... in fact, once a week, all the resorts send someone driving around to collect and return the resort bikes—only to start all over again! Our guests might take a bike ride, stop at another resort, put the bike in the bike rack (*aren't you supposed to?*), and return to no bike. I cannot tell you how many trips have been made to pick up guests, or bikes, that have been lost or misplaced. Now I brief incoming guests to either hide their bikes in the bush or just get on any bike and come home. Can you imagine in the city? Someone takes your bike, it's gone ... no trading later.

A funny story circulated soon after Peter bought Southern Cross Club, which was the very first resort on the island, built in the 1950s ... his bikes kept disappearing. Were they being put on a boat and taken to the other islands? Legend is ... he finally ran an ad in the paper asking people to PLEASE not "borrow" his bikes, and offered a reward for returned bikes. He even offered to purchase a bike for anyone who needed one ... please contact Southern Cross Club. The bikes stopped disappearing.

People "borrow" things all the time. We had a big seat that we used in the resort's 34-foot dive boat, once a year, when we went to drydock in Grand Cayman. On this single-engine boat, it was a six-hour journey, made much more pleasant with this comfortable chair. (The eighty-mile Grand Cayman trip can take between two and six hours, depending on the boat.) The rest of the year, the seat was kept in the generator storage shed. So, one day, a Bracker (a person from Cayman Brac) came over and asked if he could borrow the chair for his fishing boat. He said, "It fits perfectly in my boat." We said "No" and explained why and when we needed it. September rolled around, and we were getting ready to do the annual crossing to the marina, only to find the bench gone! We called the guy to ask if he had our bench. He answered nonchalantly, "Yes"—as if, of *course!* We asked that he return it by Saturday, because we were leaving Sunday, and if it was *not* here, we would report it as stolen to the cops and tell them we knew who the "thief" was ... it was returned Saturday. The funny twist to the story: he *is* a policeman! I still try to envision him driving up to the generator shed, loading the seat, and driving away, after being told "No". At least we had the seat for the long boat ride.

Part of the charm of Little Cayman is not having to lock your doors. As the island grows and changes, we get some amenities, but will we also experience the downside of growth? We'll see as time goes on.

Since this chapter involves transport, I thought I would mention Cuban migrants. Over the years, we have seen all manner of boats come by here, some barely afloat, sometimes with no running engine, but loaded to the gunwales with as many people as the boat can hold. Since I grew up in the U.S., I can't imagine wanting to flee a country so desperately that you would do so in a questionably seaworthy vessel, across miles of open ocean ... sometimes on hope alone.

Sometimes a boat brings people who have no permit to work in the Cayman Islands. They are supposed to check in as visitors and are given a time frame as to how long they can stay. In the early years, a boatload of Jamaicans were heard to have come ashore ... unregistered. The island official came by and asked if we had seen anyone unknown (at that time, we *did* know everyone on island!) and then left to scan the beach with his binoculars. We couldn't resist having a bit of fun. We took a pair of sandals, went down to the ocean, and walked up the beach, planting extra footsteps with the sandals, making it look like a small group had landed on our shores. Then we reported "fresh tracks". The tracks were investigated, but no fugitive Jamaicans were found—at this location.

6

Living on Island Time

Ahh ... the island life. Laid back, stress-free, this is nothing like back home! Yet, in some ways, you wish it were ...

During your quick lunch hour in Grand Cayman is when you finally get a chance to run your errands. Well, the workers in the shops, on island time, are *not* in a hurry. I have seen a clerk answer the phone and say "Hold on a minute and I'll check." As she put the customer on hold, she chatted with her fellow-worker for a couple of minutes about her night on the town, how dinner went, who all showed up, blah blah blah. After covering all of the events in detail, the clerk finally remembered the potential customer, on *hold!* I have also been on the other end of the phone during an inquiry, and actually *heard* the conversation. I was on hold so long one time, I finally resorted to yelling into the receiver, hoping she would hear me. No luck. At least in the U.S.—much as people say they hate it—you have "elevator music". Which would you rather listen to—elevator music or her night on the town?

Living on an island, we try to adjust and slow down. You may not learn to slow down, but you *do* learn to make adjustments and allow a lot more time than you might think is necessary, even to run small errands. It will *always* take more time than you think, and as Murphy's law says, "If something can go wrong, it will."

It takes a while to get used to local labor. There was the story of someone doing a job painting. The manager went out to see what was happening and found the painter motionless. When the manager asked what he was doing, he replied that he was "waiting for the paint to dry, so I can put on another coat"!

Renewing a driver's license in Grand Cayman is *known* for gobbling up a whole lunch hour. In fact, if you can go at any other time of day, it can be almost painless. My dad taught me to carry a book at all times—when you get delayed or have to wait in line, reading helps the time pass and reduces frustration. On this particular day, everything was working like clockwork. I didn't even have time to open the book ... the line was moving fast! Okay—what's the catch? Before I knew it, I had filled out the form, paid the fees, and was seated in a waiting area along with three other people. In fact, since everything had gone *so* smoothly, I jokingly said to the others that we should check to make sure we didn't get someone else's picture on our licenses. No sooner had I said this than the door opened, the gentleman's name was called, and as he stood to accept his new driver's license, he burst out laughing. Staring up at him from his new card was a lady who was in the waiting room with us. Oops! *Now* the delay starts ... take a seat, this will only take a moment ...

No matter how long we live in the islands, we're still considered "foreigners" or "expats". One reason for the delay in service is to remind us that even though we live here, we are still "visitors" to their island. A funny thing happened when I went to pick up our new mountain bikes. Ed and I had just done a mini-triathlon stateside, then shipped the bikes to the island. Your goods are received at customs, and you go to collect them and pay a twenty percent import duty on their value. The customs area was under renovation, so it was like going through a maze. I was sent from one clerk to another, one counter to the next, and at one point, even the workers seemed unsure which counter did what. Of course, as I was standing in line and going from building to building, I couldn't help but glance frequently at the wall clock. It was constantly reminding me that the customs office closed at four o'clock today, and, since it was Friday, they would be closed for the weekend. Next chance: Monday. I was seeing my chances "ticking" away as the minutes went by. The day's goal was starting to look unattainable. The other part of the equation: the resort dive boat, *Yellow Rose*, had been in the marina for its yearly maintenance, and our scheduled departure was Saturday, because weather was coming this way. The boat was how we were transporting the bikes, so I was in a bit of a hurry to complete the task. If we missed getting the bikes that day, we would have to ask someone to clear them from customs and take them to the shipping company to get them over to Little Cayman. Quite a favor to ask—plus, as you can see, it could take a lot of time to arrange!

The forms had been filed, and the final part of my journey was to go to the warehouse—a *huge*, open building. Not a soul in sight. I noticed the wall clock: 3:55. In search of an agent, I hollered out, "Hello? ... Hello!" A customs officer finally emerged from an office. Somehow, I had found the back entrance—not hard to do with renovations and no signs. The agent directed me to a fenced-off area by the office—obviously the entrance, and obviously, no one else there. It was closing time! He asked me to take a number and have a seat. I looked to both sides of me, behind me, and was still convinced there was no one else there—just him and me. But hey, he's in charge here. So, I picked a number and took a seat. This system probably works well when the waiting area is packed with people who have to pay a twenty percent duty on items shipped in from the States. There are no taxes in the Cayman Islands, so these are our "fees" for living here. The wall clock loomed just above my head as I sat, thinking that disassembling the bikes and putting them on the plane *could* work ...

All of a sudden, the man in authority yelled out "Number three!" It was my number! I glanced around excitedly, felt like I had just won the lottery, and nearly leaped out of the chair. Then I remembered ... no, I was the only one there. We proceeded to discuss the value to be assessed, I paid the fees, and I walked out with the bikes just after four o'clock. Last client of the day. Two lessons that day. They don't close exactly at four o'clock—it means "around four o'clock"—and even though we live here, it is still "their" island.

Impatience is a feeling we all know from living on an island. It is island time—we remind ourselves daily. Kelly, from Grand Cayman, tells the story of a man coming into the dive shop, sweaty and red in the face. He already felt the world was against him. He wanted to go diving. When she asked to see his diving certification card, he said he didn't have it. Kelly said he needed it to dive. He was livid. "First I go to rent a car, and they won't let me because I don't have my credit card. Now, you won't let me dive because I don't have my C card. And look at *this!*" he shouted, exposing two bloody, scratched-up forearms. Kelly looked quizzically at him. "I wanted to at least get a coconut. I climbed the tree to get one, and LOOK what it did to my arms! I HATE this island!" he yelled, as he stormed out of the dive shop.

One thing you learn quickly in the islands is ... always, always, always double-check everything. You cannot assume (and we all know what that stands for!) that just because you have ordered something, someone will follow through and send it your way. OR that the item will come as you ordered it. You could order one bottle of Grenadine, yet receive a case—or vice versa: order a case of Appleton island rum, but receive only one bottle. Go figure. (Both of these *have* happened.)

One morning, realizing that the supply barge would be delayed by weather, I called in a small produce order to help us survive until the barge came. Gladys has a reputation for great food, and we do whatever it takes to keep that standard up—even flying in the produce! Various fresh fruits, a few cases of eggs, portobello mushrooms, and a couple of heads of romaine and iceberg lettuce should cover it. I explained to the wholesaler that the items *had* to be delivered to Island Air by 12:45. Island Air is the only inter-island air service, and usually you have to charter the plane for your produce; however, this particular flight was a charter going to Little Cayman empty, returning guests to Grand Cayman. Perfect for carrying food in!

Since timing was crucial to make the charter flight, I called the wholesaler around 12:15 to make sure the items were enroute to the plane ... only to be told "We were waiting till the last minute!" Immediately, my mind played a few scenarios of the food not making the plane, running out of food for the guests, and so forth. I took a deep breath and tried to calmly explain that this was exactly what I did *not* want to happen—afraid they would miss the *only* available flight that day. Plus, the next couple of days showed full flights. The grocery clerk then explained his reasoning: he didn't want the "ice" to melt. There was silence on both ends of the phone. I knew I hadn't ordered ice ... then it finally dawned on me. When I had said "iceberg lettuce", he had heard only "ice". Then, of course, my mind went one step further. In fact, let me ask you. If you were a clerk taking the order and saw "ice" on the list, wouldn't you call and double-check? Envision the ice being delivered at 12:30 on a hot airport tarmac, waiting to leave on a flight "around" 12:45, spending forty minutes on the plane, and then being collected in Little Cayman. I wonder what state the ice would be in. Luckily, since I thought to follow up on it, we ended up with iceberg lettuce instead of a puddle, formerly ice.

In Little Cayman, you forgo shopping, night life, crowds, amenities (though swimming pools and satellite TV are here now!), and even mail service. Since we are the smallest of the three Cayman Islands, you might say we are the last stop on the block. I received one letter three *years* after it was mailed. In fact, over the years I had wondered why the guy had not responded to my letters. He had—and when the letter finally arrived, it was easy to understand the delay: it had stamps from traveling all over the world! Everywhere in the world that had an "I" in the address. Instead of Islands, it was missent to Iceland and Ireland, and had the postal stamps from both those places. I still have the envelope. Classic!

Christmas mail in May is another favorite. In other words, don't mail homemade cookies to your friends in the islands—they may not arrive in an edible state! This has happened more than once.

Claudette, who lives on Cayman Brac, had been to visit her brother in North Carolina and was bringing back stone-ground grits for herself and a Southern friend. Her brother worked with a guy whose brother runs an art gallery in Grand Cayman, and she was asked to bring back a bag of grits for him. When she got back to the Brac, she called the gallery and got the mailing address, packaged up the grits, and sent them off to Grand Cayman. This was in July. Her brother came to visit her in early December. He had to spend a few hours in Grand Cayman, so he arranged to deliver some grits to the art-gallery owner, because the grits Claudette had sent had never gotten there. They eventually did ... the week after Christmas. Ninety miles away ... five months in transit ... where WERE they?

Sally, who worked at one of the resorts, had gone to Grand Cayman for the day to shop and buy gardening items, among other errands. Since the plane charges fifty cents a pound for any cargo over fifty-five pounds per person (which, after a day of shopping, she had), she decided it would be cheaper to mail herself the potting soil. You can mail up to twenty-one pounds for four dollars. The bag of soil weighed twenty pounds. To put it on the plane as excess weight would have cost ten dollars. So she saved six dollars, and it came on the same plane anyway—just in the mailbag instead of in a suitcase. What a laugh!

I believe my all-time favorite was when the mailbag fell out of—or off of—the plane. It's unclear whether the mailbag was put in the luggage compartment and the door wasn't shut completely *or* the bag was placed on a wing and forgotten as other bags were being loaded. Stuff happens. In any case, Terry was on a day off, reading on the porch of a house that overlooks the Booby Pond. He heard the plane passing over and glanced up in time to see something drop toward the pond. His first thought, he said, was that the plane had hit a bird. Later in the day, Neil, the policeman, came to the local watering hole, the Hungry Iguana, and asked if anyone had any knowledge of what had happened. Terry led them to the dripping mailbag—and then became an eyewitness for the investigation that ensued. Postal officials flew in from Grand Cayman. Big event! The worst part was that some people were inconvenienced because passports or money for bills didn't reach their destination—the items were being held as evidence.

Since there is a time delay on mail, Pirates Point has learned that the fastest way to get U.S.-bound mail out is to give it, stamped and sealed, to a departing guest, who hand-carries it Stateside and posts it for us. It can be a bit confusing to our future guests, who get confirmations of their reservations from different U.S. states! So ... we observe all week and try to send the mail with someone who seems responsible. One week, I chose Tim.[11] I gave him a big envelope that contained all the U.S. mail, stamped, and explained that all he had to do was empty the contents of the envelope into any U.S. mailbox. About a week later, the owner, Gladys, was hollering at me, "Why did you ask that guy to send the U.S. mail *back* to us?!" What? Of course I didn't ask him to do that! He had sealed the big brown envelope, added postage, and returned it to us here in Little Cayman. Honestly! ... he *looked* smart and responsible. Oh well ...

better luck next time.

The next week, the same thing happened again—only this time, Gladys was involved. She gave the U.S. mail to Stuart.[12] He was dropped off at Little Cayman's airport to await his plane. About ten minutes later, we received a phone call from Leonie, the local postmistress, who was going on and on about something. Finally, the phone was passed to me, to decipher what had happened. I got off the phone, laughing, and asked Gladys, "Why did you ask that guy to send the U.S. mail back to us from Little Cayman?" Of course, she hadn't. He had taken the brown envelope to the local post office, and Miss Leonie was calling to tell us how much Cayman Islands postage would be required to mail the contents from here! The letters already *had* U.S. postage—just confusion on *where* to mail them, this time ...

All post offices have special seasonal stamps printed up, and I'm sure people have seen Christmas stamps used after the season. Bob and Janet, from England, who used to live here in the early 1990s and returned in 2000 to buy a condo, told me they had purchased Christmas stamps in 1996, returned to England, and then noticed that the stamps had a 1992 date on them. I'm sure there are stacks of "surprise" stamps in every post office. The interesting thing is that the postal rates had not gone up in those four years!

Everyone fantasizes about life on an island. That's why so many people say "I would love to live here" or "I would love to do what you do." Yes, when you're on vacation, it *is* relaxing—hammocks, sunshine, ocean breeze. It can't get much better than this ... true. But when you live here and work at a resort, or own a house that you come down to every so often, there is a lot to accomplish—and we have the same twenty-four hours you do back home. The salt air is constantly generating maintenance problems. The local vegetation and weeds are continually encroaching on your piece of property. In other words, there is upkeep, just like at home. However, we do learn to have fun and enjoy the island—we try to slow down and enjoy the view.

Speaking of views, one of the common questions we get asked is "Do you get the green flash?" Yes, we do. A definition: green flash is caused by the atmosphere bending or refracting the shorter wavelengths more than the longer ones. When the sun touches the horizon, the longer red wavelengths go above the observer, but the shorter green ones are bent, so the sun appears green.

In the earlier years here, before there were any condos or homes, there were a few challenges. Water was never overly abundant. Bob and Janet Freemantle lived here in those years and said doing laundry was a nightmare. "We were usually short of water, so I had to cycle it in the 'communal' washing machine. Sometimes, if the lid was left up, nature added things to the wash. Very often clothes were left in the machine, but—because the population was so small—it was easy to recognize whose they were because we had seen them wearing those clothes. Water was sometimes recycled: the rinse water became the wash water for the next load. All our clothes were the same color: island gray!"

Earlier, I mentioned house maintenance. Rick and Crystal Jones had come down and were doing the standard catch-up on their house and yard work. Most residents say it takes them the first couple of weeks to get the house in order, then they can relax and enjoy. Next door to the Joneses, a house was being renovated. Living out near the end of the island at Point of Sand, they were not used to seeing many other people. As Rick would grab a drink and sit on the porch for a quick break, he would see the worker, Ron Sefton, waving at him. He'd wave back and then move on to his next task. A little later, the scene was repeated. After a couple of times, Rick said he thought that was the friendliest worker he'd ever seen. As he grabbed binoculars it dawned on him: Ron wasn't waving to be friendly, he was waving because he needed help—his ladder had fallen away from the second story where he was working.

Ken and Louise Wagnon have one of the most beautiful custom-built homes on the island. It has an area for dive gear with a rinse tank, a gorgeous landscaped yard with flowering plumeria and various shades of bougainvillea, and a cobblestone driveway. It has hurricane shutters that drop down to cover the large oceanside viewing windows when the Wagnons leave the island. Theirs is a very detailed and obviously well-planned home. Beach sand was brought in and is kept weed-free and immaculate. A hammock for watching sunsets completes the ambience. We heard that Ken's brother had come down to use the house and mentioned that there needed to be a rock to watch sunsets from … and he had found "The Rock" for five hundred dollars. Ken went ahead and purchased "The Rock"; however, by the time it was brought down the island in a front-end loader and driven down the beach, it ended up costing five thousand dollars! At least, that's the story that was handed down to me. Anyway, knowing this was a sore spot with

Ken, the next time he dove with us, Barry,[13] a fellow boat captain, decided to tease Ken. As we drove by his house enroute to the dive site, Barry said, "Beautiful beach, Ken, but that rock has got to go!" There was dead silence, and then Ken said, "I *own* "The Rock". In fact, Ken proposed to Louise on "The Rock", as they refer to it.

Sometimes people wonder what we do on islands after the sun sets. Happy hour at a place where the sunset can be watched is a favorite pastime. When I worked in Grand Cayman, the Royal Palms bar was a popular spot (until the hotel burned down in 1987). Don Foster's had six beautiful dive boats moored out front, and as the sun went down, the pink and coral shades of the sky formed a beautiful backdrop for the boats.

The boats were tied up for the night and, come morning, were brought into the beach to load up for diving. I overheard a lady at the bar one night, saying in a concerned voice, "Don't you think someone should go check on the divers?" Since she wasn't speaking specifically to me, I thought she might know about some night shore divers. When she repeated the question in a louder voice, I had to ask, "What divers?" she pointed to the six boats and said, "They've been out there a *long* time." As a boat captain, I felt it was my obligation to explain to her that there were no divers, and the boats had been put to sleep for the night. Worry not.

Another favorite pastime is night diving. I recall a story about a small group on a night dive. One man had seen a huge lobster walking around ... he got so excited, he went to clang on his tank to call the others over to see. For the rest of the week, he couldn't sit down to eat. He had used his dive knife to clang on his tank—but he missed the tank and stabbed a hole in his butt!

On almost any island, reading is a popular activity. Books are traded and shared, which can create a quick bond between people. Sue B. and her husband had come to the resort for a week. Since Sue dives and Buddy doesn't, he spent a lot of time reading, napping—and sometimes getting restless. We had a laugh when, one day, he was spotted in the hammock reading an article on menopause. Maybe he had *too* much time on his hands ...

In Little Cayman, you learn to make your own entertainment. In the earlier years, when there were only about fifteen residents, Gladys had decided to go treasure hunting. She was in charge of the expedition, Steve[14] had the metal detector, and Tom had the shovel. They had read that pirates buried their treasure under graves, so they went near (not *into*) the cemetery. Steve would swing the magic wand, and a ticking noise would indicate "treasure"! Tom would dig, and then Steve would check again. Still ticking ... dig again. This went on for quite some time. When the hole was a couple of feet deep, there still wasn't a sign of a gold doubloon. Gladys finally realized that the metal detector was picking up the shovel, where it lay at the side of the hole. Too funny.

Sometimes the barge dictates our after-hours activities. I had received an order of roses one week, to add to my garden. At eleven p.m. we were unpacking the roses to make sure they had made it okay from Grand Cayman. A temporary cop was filling in for a month, and you should have seen his face. He kept looking at us, looking at his watch, trying to figure out why anyone would be gardening that late. Hey—at least we weren't out causing trouble!

Gladys likes to entertain her guests and has a wide variety of videos available for viewing after dinner. Some of the videos are for entertainment and others are educational films about the Cayman Islands. One particular week, Gladys had a new National Trust video that she wanted to show to our dive group. Larry had been by during the day, and we had been talking about the group, and I said she would probably show the tape that night. So he substituted another tape. Gladys got in front of the video player and was excitedly talking as she punched the "play" button. She had her back to the screen but suddenly realized the music was wrong—and saw the open mouths of the guests as they watched nude bodies in bed. "Where do we sign up?" they laughingly asked. Gladys screamed "Ed!" as she tried to stop the machine— my husband always gets called to help out with the VCR. The joke of the day was the campaign to support the National Thrust.

It is inevitable that living on a small island would involve cleaning up the beaches. In the spring, we celebrate Earth Week by collecting bags and bags of trash from the beach and roadside, and there are prizes for different categories of debris. Have you ever noticed what washes up on beaches? If you see an ad in a magazine showing a pristine beach, the photo must have been taken right after a clean-up! It never ceases to amaze me: needles, vials, pieces of plastic of every color, tennis shoes and sandals (but always only one of a pair—darn!), light bulbs (unbroken!), even refrigerators. I have seen a full-size refrigerator and one of those college dorm–size ones ... go figure. A lot of our beach debris floats in from Jamaica, judging by the labels. There must be a lot of crying kids there, because one of the most common pieces of flotsam is … doll parts. You *never* find a full doll, only parts. And yes, there have been many bottles with messages inside. Some we had to translate from Spanish. Others were class projects; in those cases we sent a post-card telling the class the date we found it, so they could figure out how long it took to get here, and where "here" was. A couple of the bottles were actually thrown from the decks of cruiseships, with the date enclosed but no way of contacting the bottle-thrower. Luckily, none of them had any kind of message asking for help!

Thinking of beach clean-ups reminds me of a story passed on about a yard boy. He had climbed *way* up into a tall palm tree to trim the fronds. As he sat on a frond, hacking away with a machete, some expats were observing from the bar. There were some mumbled bets about what was going to happen next. The young boy would lean across and slice another frond loose with his sharp machete, then another, and another, until … yes, you guessed it! He sliced the one he was sitting on and tumbled to the ground amid suppressed laughter in the background.

On one of my own beach clean-ups, I had the help of one of our workers, Amy. We had loaded "tons" of palm fronds and were driving them off to the town dump. It was a horribly windy day, so Amy (all of five feet tall) offered to ride on top to help weigh down the fronds. I had repeatedly looked in the rearview mirror and caught glimpses of Amy's blond hair being tousled by the wind. At the dump, I made a wide turn and started backing up. I hollered out the window to get help from Amy, but after hearing no response, I finally got out of the truck, only to realize Amy wasn't there! I drove back on the road and arrived just in time to see her dusting off her britches. I had underestimated the strength of the wind. It had picked her and quite a few palm fronds out of the truck and deposited both of them in the middle of the road.

On another day, as I was unloading yard debris from my truck, I observed how one local guy tried to find a new way to empty his truck. I seemed to be doing it the old-fashioned way—shovelful by shovelful. So I watched curiously, as he would turn around at the far end of the dump, put the truck in reverse, stomp on the accelerator, cover the distance to where I sat, then slam on the brakes ... the idea was for all the contents to go spilling out the back of the truck. Needless to say, it did *not* work. So he would change gears, go back to the other end, and try again with the quick reverse and slam to a halt. He repeated this procedure four times while *I* was there, and when I drove away, he was *still* trying this new technique. To me, the waste of time, plus burning up four good tires, hardly seemed worth it. Yet maybe he was just having some fun!

Speaking of the town dump ... we had some Grand Cayman residents who had come to Little Cayman for a day trip. As they were getting ready to go on the island tour, they had one request: they wanted to go to the dump! They wanted to see the chickens and roosters that they had heard so much about. That was a new one for me. I know people come here for the phenomenal diving, small-resort atmosphere, and nature ... but to see the chickens at the dump? Apparently one of the women knew every type of chicken and was curious about which ones we had, but I was already mentally creating a new brochure on Little Cayman—with roosters and chickens on the cover!

While we're on the subject of island time, we can't forget the trials and tribulations of building here. What a challenge! J.J. and B.J. Ranna built a house overlooking Owen Island—a spectacular view. A few years later, Gladys was deciding to add four oceanfront rooms to the original six rooms of Pirates Point. J.J. had come to dinner and heard of Gladys's plans. He asked her point-blank, "Do you drink much, Gladys?" She replied, "A few glasses of wine with dinner, why?" His response: "If you're going to build in Little Cayman, you *will* start drinking!"

Someone else had recently had air conditioning installed in their home. They were here in the summer months and were thrilled to have a way to cool off … however, after the air conditioner had been running for *hours*, it didn't feel very different in the room. *Is the air conditioning okay? Are there any windows open?* As the owner glanced out the window, he sadly saw the reason: the insulation was standing next to the building, instead of having been put in the wall!

When John and Marilyn Palmer's house was going up in the early 1980s, they would periodically see the workers sitting around as a group. When they asked what was going on, the group reply was "We're taking a coffee break." But … there wasn't a coffeepot or cup in sight! They also remember mixing cement by hand, because no mixer was here yet. It took over a year to complete the house.

For anyone living or building here before 1992, when central power was put in, it was like pioneering days. We had generators providing the resorts with power, and when Ed and I would go home at the end of the day, we would start up the generator at home, too.

Two of the earliest non-Caymanian settlers here were Basil and Brigitte Kassa. Most people left Little Cayman after the 1932 hurricane and moved to Cayman Brac, whose topography provides more protection from storms. From 1960, there were about ten local people here, basically living off the land. But the locals know the island. The ones who interest me are those who transplanted themselves here and learned to survive and thrive.

Basil had met Brigitte when she owned a nightclub in Monte Carlo. She described those days as "glamorous and glittery" and mentioned quite a few famous names. In fact, when she first came here in 1972, she had the fancy dresses and high heels—she has now traded them for island wear. Basil and Brigitte had ordered lumber to build their house, and it had disappeared three separate times. There was no supply ship, and Brigitte remembers the crew hauling bags of cement on their shoulders, wading ashore from the small boat that carried the building supplies to Little Cayman. They first built a small house to live in while they built the main house—which took three years to complete, because they would work hard on it for a while and then travel for a while. So as not to lose any of the materials, they chartered a boat from Florida, with a ramp that pulled right up to their property. They brought their own tractor and crane to haul supplies and cement blocks around. Generators provided power, and workmen were brought over from the Brac—and housed and fed—to do the labor. The house, which is 120 feet long, has a *huge* open living room, walk-in closets lined with cedar, and beautiful, ornate tiles, some of them handpainted, on the kitchen and bathroom walls.. When you see the collection of items from Bali, Cuba, Hong Kong, Italy, and other exotic places, you have to remind yourself that you're actually in Little Cayman!

When I asked Brigitte about the contrast between "glittery" and down-to-earth, she said that going from one extreme to the other was a challenge for her. In the earlier years, living and building here and enjoying it *were* the challenge. She did well with plants, but early on a lack of fresh water was a hardship, so her house has a 75,000-gallon cistern to catch rainwater. Zinnias, cockscomb, salvia, and many colors of roses line her walkway.

When power came to Little Cayman in 1992, Basil and Brigitte had the first TV. Naturally, everyone wanted to know what was happening out in the "real" world. People told of seeing Basil on the tractor, driving around and around Southern Cross Club, hollering out the latest news. This got him dubbed "Mr. Cronkite". Basil has since passed on, but the memory remains.

The Southern Cross Club was the first resort on Little Cayman. In 1958, Dr. Logan Robertson, from North Carolina, and some investors created a private fishing camp: ten rooms in wooden buildings. Sometimes, when whole families came during summer camps, tents were pitched on the grounds for the overflow. Weather and termites took their toll, and in 1971 the wooden buildings were torn down and replaced with the poured concrete structures that are still around today. Southern Cross remained an invitation-only private club until

1981, when Kent Howard and thirty-four shareholders bought out the original investors. As the 1980s rolled around, Mike Emmanuelle, who had been around the camp for a while already, decided to bring scuba diving to Little Cayman. There may have been dive boats from Cayman Brac doing day trips here, but this was considered the beginning of Little Cayman's land-based operations.

In 1995, Southern Cross Club was taken to a new level of success by Peter Hillenbrand. He purchased the resort and put untold amounts of money into renovations ... and it shows. Their focus is still fishing and diving, though.

One house on Little Cayman was built specifically as an experimental home. Ed Ball, who invented the Ball canning jar and later moved into space-age materials, brought in special materials to see if they could withstand hurricanes and termites. His house was built in the 1960s, and he thought it would last forever. Ha! The house was basically gutted and rebuilt in the late '90s. To build on Little Cayman requires an adventurous spirit. Once you're established, though, you feel it was well worth the few inconveniences that are inevitable when you choose to build on a small, remote island.

7

Supply & Demand:
Culinary Delights & Mishaps

*I*n earlier chapters, you were introduced to the supply barge that brings the necessities to us. In Little Cayman, it's easy to see how sometimes the supply could be "neck and neck" with consumption. Even when I lived in Grand Cayman, there were times when the store shelves were nearly empty because huge container ships couldn't dock or offload their cargo. Strong nor'westers hit the islands in winter, much like the winter storms that paralyze cities in the States. Huge waves come crashing into the main harbor in Grand Cayman, flooding the waterfront streets. The supply boats and barges go into a holding pattern on the opposite side of the island. Once the weather passes, the containers are dispersed to wholesalers and super-markets, which then deliver their orders to the waiting restaurants and resorts, which can then prepare meals for their patrons and guests. The time between famine and feast reminds us that we live on an island and are truly at the mercy of the weather.

Moving to Little Cayman made me even more aware of the cycle of food needs. At Pirates Point, one of the main attractions (and a good part of our reputation) is that we're on a remote island and yet serve food that is regularly touted as some of the best in the Cayman Islands. The resort and its food were even listed in *100 Best Resorts in the Caribbean*, by Kay Showker. Needless to say, that reputation constitutes a challenge. Fresh produce, fresh fish, and homemade breads and desserts are part of what make up three gourmet meals each day. Cam and Dianne are the two chefs who create the menus and food, dependent on the supplies at hand. They've become very adept at substituting for ingredients that didn't arrive and ensuring an outstanding meal every time. We know the number of guests inhouse, and daily add outside dinner guests who have made reservations ahead of time. Since everything is homemade and takes quite a bit of prep time, we don't cater to walk-in guests. There's no menu to order from ... once the food is prepared, it is served buffet-style, and table by table, the guests are served and can return for seconds—or thirds. We alternate between fish and various meats, to give guests variety throughout the week.

On one of our particularly busy nights, we were just about to serve dinner when we turned around and saw *six* unannounced people in the lobby. Cam was hoping we hadn't made a mistake in the dinner count, because he had the exact number of desserts. When we offered to help them (*do they need T-shirts, do they want to see a room?*), they asked for a menu! Wrong resort—wrong concept! In fact, in Little Cayman, the Hungry Iguana/Paradise Villas is the only restaurant that you can walk into, without a reservation, and order off a menu. The other three resorts, like ours, operate with a buffet service, and the meal head count is known ahead of time.

Breakfast is also a buffet: homemade granola, yogurt, fresh fruit, bagels, English muffins, and a main dish, which alternates between various egg dishes (eggs benedict or huevos rancheros, for instance) and homemade french toast, waffles, or pancakes. One morning, a guest asked, "What kind of eggs do you have?" The staff, who have all been here a while, were thinking, a bit sarcastically, *iguana, fish, turtle* ... Trying to suppress a laugh and seeing the customer's questioning look, we just responded, "Scrambled."

In the earlier years, before we had a corner grocery store, we learned to be really self-sufficient. In fact, one of our recipes calls for green papayas, which are gathered on the island. Not much else is grown here, so we depended on careful wholesale ordering and bringing many items in on each return trip from the States. Nuts, chocolates, kitchen utensils, spices, and other items that either can't be found in the islands or are prohibitively expensive were brought in, in huge "whale" duffel bags. I can remember Gladys bringing five or six of these bags, each weighing seventy to eighty pounds, full of essential ingredients.

Another source of supplies is the repeat guests. This system is still in place today. They will call up, ask what we need, and bring in an item or two. We might ask for a truck part, an egg-decorating kit for Easter, candles for birthday cakes, or white chocolate for baking desserts. The participation gives people a sense of adventure when they talk to their friends back home, who are asking, "You're taking *what*? To *where*?"

Without these systems, people on staff would start to crave certain things. I had to laugh the first time I saw a Domino's hot-pack pizza delivery bag on the plane from Grand Cayman! (At Pirates Point we make home-made pizza once a week because we *know* guests start missing their comfort foods!) At one point, it became a weekly thing. Harry[15] would call around, get the orders, pick up the pizzas at the airport, and distribute them from the store. Imagine the poor passengers, smelling the pizzas the whole flight—what torture!

When the store first came to Little Cayman in 1993, a funny story made the rounds. It seems that the manager walked away, locked the door, ran an errand, and returned to the store only to see someone with his face plastered against the glass, banging and hollering, afraid he had been locked in to spend the night! People got so excited to have choices, after having nothing for years, they would spend ages in the store. Nowadays the options—mail order, specialty stores, shopping trips to a Walmart in the States—boggle the mind. People take for granted what they have ...

Now that you know a bit about the great food at the resort, you can imagine our shock when a guest arrived and said, "Is this *it*?" Unsure what the problem was, we had to ask what it was he needed. He said he was used to steak and lobster every night in *his* restaurant back home! Well, we do not do steaks ("too plebeian," Gladys says) and it wasn't lobster season, so she gave him a challenge: "If you bring it in, we'll cook it." He chartered a plane to go to Grand Cayman, with his wife, nanny, and child, and they returned with steaks, hot dogs, and Sara Lee cakes (in preference to our homemade ones!). He also ordered a *case* of Maine lobster to be flown into Little Cayman. The air freight bill alone was nine hundred dollars. We borrowed a *huge* barbecue grill/cooker and proceeded to grill lobster. Everyone had their fill, and for the rest of the week we had lobster salads and lobster appetizers. The funny part was that word got around the island that Pirates Point was having a lobster cookout— was it Caribbean lobster, caught illegally off-season? Hearsay was that the island official was surprised to see lobster claws at the town dump. (Local lobsters don't have claws.) Pirates Point is extremely conservation-minded—we constantly educate divers and work with them to minimize damage to the reef. Going out and getting lobster off-season would never have crossed our minds.

Holidays take a bit of extra planning. You need to order far enough ahead to assure that the Butterball turkeys will make it here from Grand Cayman ... not be stuck in a container because of weather. Since they take up so much freezer space, however, we don't want them *too* soon! Every year Gladys brings in smoked turkey and smoked ham from Texas. The fresh produce—green beans, cranberries, etc.—comes from the big island. Our homemade breads have been turned into dressings, and Thanksgiving is truly a feast. I think it is one of people's favorite meals—plus, you can eat to excess and nobody's watching!

One Thanksgiving, Cam, who has been the chef for the past five years, began trying to get his turkeys into Little Cayman. Here's how the drill works: when a shipment is coming in, first we're given the shipping/landing papers, which tell us what items have come to the island. Then we go to the containers to unload produce, frozen foods, beer, sodas, and so forth. We have repeatedly asked the suppliers to mark each box "Pirates Point" so that it is easier when it arrives. I'm not sure they understand how it is on the receiving end of cargo. Sometimes pallets shift or break open, and there is a hodge-podge pile of supplies with five resorts trying to get their items as quickly as possible so we can get on with the day's events. Multi-tasking is a well-used word here. This particular day, the sea conditions were rough and the tug and barge were in a hurry to leave, so we quickly packed the truck "to the gunnels" with fresh produce and drove back to the resort. We unloaded the cases of lettuce, portobello mushrooms, radicchio, fennel, snow peas, and fresh fruits—kiwi, pineapples, mangoes, honeydew melons, and strawberries. Cam and Curtis, the other chef at that time, began putting the produce into the huge three-door commercial Victory refrigerators, while we returned for the frozen items. Once the items are put away, the food is checked off on the produce invoice. Every week, there is a mistake. An item may be on the list but didn't arrive, OR we might have received twenty potatoes, listed as twenty *cases*. At 589 Cayman dollars, that's $718 U.S. for potatoes! *Excuse me—we need a credit!* You can *never* assume it's correct.

When we returned to the dock, knowing by the paperwork that we had frozen food to pick up, there was no barge—and no containers left unopened. Empty containers were gaping at us. There was *nothing* left! As had happened in the past, we thought maybe someone had mistakenly loaded our frozen items into a waiting truck along with theirs. It's usually pretty busy, and as we're passing cases "chain gang" style, nothing really gets checked off the invoices until we return to the resort. Plus, on summer days when the sun is beating down on the produce, it's best to get everything refrigerated, *then* check off the list.

So I went back to the resort to make a few phone calls. I called every resort in Cayman Brac and the other resorts in Little Cayman, in search of not only two twenty-pound Butterball turkeys but our *whole* frozen-food order—bacon, English muffins, bagels, and our meat for the week. Since it was Sunday, the shipping company was not reachable by phone—so I researched what I could, to find out that—yep, we were still missing the turkeys. On Monday, I reported the missing frozen-food order, only to be told it must be in the Sister Islands somewhere. Nope! I hinted that maybe it was still in the container. The barge had left in a hurry—in fact, the captain didn't even take empty containers back with him to the big island. I was assured it was *not* in Grand Cayman but in someone else's fridge. Finally, on Tuesday, we received a call from an embarrassed shipping-company employee that the meats and other items had been found—you guessed it—in a container in Grand Cayman, days later! Apparently, the guy who drives the containers on and off the barge had seen us leave with our truck full of produce. In his haste to leave because of the weather, he assumed we were done, slammed the doors without looking inside, and off they went into the sunset. The container, after leaving here, became unrefrigerated and sat on the dock for a couple of days. You could guess what our turkeys looked like … in fact, do you think they located them by smell? Yuk!

Since it wasn't our fault, and by now we had consumed a good percentage of the food in the time spent locating the missing items, the shipping company kindly put bacon, English muffins, and the things we were desperate for on the plane, to get us by until the next barge. The next barge arrived, turkeys intact, the day *before* Thanksgiving. That's shaving it a little too close for comfort. That is the biggest challenge on a remote island … getting the things you need *when* you need them.

Being on land is challenge enough, but Dianne, our

latest and greatest chef, used to work on a liveaboard boat. She tells hilarious stories of the food not making it to the dock and having to be shuttled to the liveaboard in a small skiff. Water-makers are crucial for this type of operation, and she has many stories of boiling food in sea water when there was no fresh water to be had ... "water-maker's down again". Then there are the challenges of cooking in rough sea conditions. *Everything* shifts, and opening the refrigerator door is like opening a shaken-up Coke can—you never know what's going to fall out. Even the stove threatened to spit out pans of lasagne, so Dianne would sit in a chair and hold the stove door shut to keep the food from hitting the floor. Also, in rough-water conditions people's desire to be on a liveaboard would dwindle, and Dianne would get approached by desperate customers, faces greenish with seasickness, a MasterCard or Visa in their outstretched hand: "*Please* get me off this boat *now*! I'll pay *any* amount!"

Sometimes, when items don't make their destination, it's *not* the shipping company's fault. I was headed to the village one day (sounds like "willage" when spoken by locals), behind a haphazardly loaded truck. Trailing slowly behind it, I had to slam on my brakes to avoid colliding with an object as it smashed to the ground. As I stopped to help, I realized there wasn't much I could do—the label on the box read FRAGILE: EGGS!

Since we are a ten-room resort and operate with a small staff, barge day always poses complications. Multi-tasking is part of the deal. Hearing the plane arrive, I stopped unloading supplies for the moment and drove to the airport to pick up our new guests, a father-and-son team. After a short orientation—to welcome them, offer them food and drinks, and tell them to make themselves at home—I went back to unpack boxes. Since we were a bit short-handed that day, I was a T-shirt salesclerk, phone reservationist, and bartender to walk-in guests. (Our inhouse guests have self-service permission in the bar. We want them to feel as though they are in a private home, which they are!) I finally got back to working on the barge order, only to see the son with his head stuck into the kitchen, saying, "'Scuse me ... we have a problem with the bathroom." At this point in the day, I can envision an overflowing toilet, a burst water pipe ... whatever. As we walked away from the weekly supply pile and headed down the hall, he repeated and clarified the problem: "There's a lizard in the bathroom!" A baby iguana had somehow found his way into the sink bowl, but since the sides were slippery, he couldn't get a foothold to escape. That was *much* easier to fix than a clogged toilet—and much more pleasant.

Speaking of fixing things ... I think that, when we call suppliers to order even *new* items, they decide, "Hey, it's going out of the country, so the warranty will be invalid. Let's send them the 'lemon' that we haven't been able to get rid of!" Seriously, it is an ongoing problem. The resort ordered a brand-new (locals say "new brand") Champion dishwasher. Excellent. After the first few washings, we noticed that it was doing a horrible job, not even cleaning the plates. This was its first few loads—there should be *no* problems. Soon it was discovered that the machine comes with an "optional" feature: to add soap! Now does *that* makes sense? Would you think, in buying a *commercial* dishwasher, that you would need to buy the soap-filling option? What next?!

As you can see, the challenges of doing gourmet meals in a remote resort are continual. Gladys, Cam, and Dianne do a fine job of making it happen—daily. To share a few of the delights, I have chosen some dishes that have won first or second place at our annual Little Cayman Cook-off in the spring. You might want to be here on island for the next one!

- Four-layer Ghirardelli chocolate cake: a Kahlua cheesecake bottom, then cream cheese and cake layers, topped with whipped cream and chocolate shavings
- Curried wahoo stuffed in avocado
- Grilled lobster salad with fennel
- Jerk pork tenderloin with caribe sauce
- Three-cheese tortellini with shrimp and lump crab-meat in a parmesan cream sauce

In the old days in the Islands, the people cooked using a "caboose". A caboose consisted of a wooden frame on legs, filled with sand. Dry wood would be put in a hole in the sand, lit, and allowed to burn down to coals. The pot containing the food would then be buried and covered with burning coals, or hung over the coals to simmer, and cooked for as long as necessary.

Valda S. is a Caymanian lady who has been a maid at Pirates Point for the past nine years. She knows how to cook! Valda's husband, Johnny, is a great fisherman who keeps the fresh-caught fish coming—and Caymanians love their fish. Following are a couple of ways to cook fish Cayman-style.[16]

Fish (wahoo, tuna, queen triggerfish)

Wash fish with lime. Then cut up the fish and pour over it oil and vinegar, seasonings, and melted margarine. Broil or steam over a slow fire. You can add sweet peppers and onions, and even a hot pepper, if you want.

For stewed fish (also called coconut dinner or rundown), open a brown coconut. Put the coconut meat in a blender, then squeeze out the milk and boil it down. Add 2 tablespoons of flour and mix in whatever chopped vegetables you want, and then add the fish. Cook slowly till fish is flaky and vegetables are tender.

Whelks

Whelks (or "wilks", as they are called locally) are small snails found along the shoreline. They have to be boiled until tender and then picked out of the shell (a tedious job!). Then they are cut up into tiny morsels and cooked with bacon, seasonings, and coconut milk—bliss!

A typical Caymanian meal includes fish or meat; white rice, rice and red beans (called "rice and peas"), or mashed potatoes; mixed vegetables (corn, peas, carrots, green beans), fried ripe plantain (looks like a big banana, but *must* be cooked before eating or you get a tummy-ache!), fried bread or "johnny-cakes", and usually a starchy root vegetable like cassava or yam.

A favorite traditional dessert is called "heavy cake" ... and believe me, it is! Not only is the pot heavy, this dessert stays with you awhile! You have to remember that in earlier years, there was little or no imported food and people worked very hard, so they needed food that would keep them full for a long time. Heavy cake was invented by past grandmothers, and the recipes have been passed on orally through the generations. (A quick aside: Caymanians prefer the meat and milk of brown coconuts to those of green ones. They say brown ones taste better. You can learn to tell whether a coconut is green or brown by the weight: the green ones feel heavier. Now you have a challenge for your next island visit!)

Heavy cake

Into a big round pot with a tight-fitting lid, put coconut milk (see recipe for fish), cinnamon, nutmeg (freshly grated if possible), margarine, raisins, and brown sugar. Then add your main ingredient; it could be yam, cassava, squash (which the islanders call "pumpkin"), macaroni, or papaya (which *must* have cornstarch added with it). The amounts depend on how many you are feeding. Mix all the ingredients together and put the lid on the pot. Bake the cake in a slow oven (formerly they were baked in the caboose) for two and a half hours.

As you wait impatiently to taste the cake, you might hear a local saying: "Soon come." I don't think I need to translate that!

Obviously, cooks and chefs want to be proud of what they present as a finished product. But sometimes even they have a bad day. One chef who shall remain anonymous told of getting ready for a Christmas Cook-off. The resort had entered a conch chowder with New England crabmeat and it had been cooking on a slow burner all day. All of a sudden realizing that time was running out, the chef got in a hurry and turned up the heat ... only to scorch the entry. Maybe next year!

Another chef I know was a fantastic baker. His cookies and cakes were to die for. He was making a special birthday cake. He had just moved to Little Cayman and was getting used to the differences between a convection and a regular oven, and the specifics of cooking at sea level. In horror, he opened the oven to find a collapsed chocolate cake! Gladys realized she would have to save the day—so she "threw" icing on the cake, five minutes before our presentation with candles and cameras flashing. As we shuffled embarrassedly into the dining room, I heard Gladys say, "Now, for an Aggie's birthday you have to make an Aggie cake." As we put the saddest-looking birthday cake I have ever seen in front of the guy, the room *erupted* with howls of laughter. That was the most photographed cake ever—and Gladys pulled it off!

Here's a look at what goes on behind the scenes in a resort kitchen. Although we never cook for large numbers of people, since everything is hand-done and homemade, the food we serve does involve extra preparation time. Also, because our guests bond with us, they want to have those special celebrations with us—birthdays, anniversaries, even weddings. It can become busy, and sometimes, cooking under warm, humid conditions in a tight time frame can cause the "cake dance" to occur ... pans are crashing, flour is coating the floor, and expletives are flying as the heat starts to melt the icing on the three-tiered wedding cake. By the time the cake goes out front to the dining room, it's not only a gourmet delight but a visual extravaganza, with icing piped around the edges and multicolored flowers cascading off the top tier. The staff has survived another cake dance.

As the island grows, more receptions and teas are held for visiting VIPs. At one reception for a former Governor, Little Cayman's residents—even the seven island children and their teacher—had shown up to honor him. Everyone was grazing on the buffet, and, of course, the children's plates were full of every type of cookie available. The teacher warned them that they needed to eat more than just cookies. The children's response: "Yes, ma'am. We waitin' for them to cut the cake!"

Another former Governor was known for being prim and slightly stuffy. A guest at Southern Cross Club, in the lobby making a phone call home, had really gotten into the relaxed island style. He had his bare feet up on the desk and was reclining in an easy chair, talking about how nice it was to be here. A nicely dressed man came through the front door. The guest was surprised to see someone so formally attired. As the gentleman paused to be greeted at the door by someone, the guest had to ask, "Who are you?" The man grandly replied, "I'm the Governor of the Cayman Islands." The disbelieving guest got back on the phone to his friend back home and was explaining whom he had just met, but his comment was "He thinks he's the f—-ing Governor!" He was!

8

Dive Instructor–
Student Funnies

"Do you live here?" "How do you become a dive instructor? I'd *love* to do what you do!"

In all seriousness, I love what I do for a living. When I went away to college, my interests were music and sports. At the university, I spent half my time in a piano practice room and the other half on sports and other physical activities—racquetball, running, ballroom dancing, and *always* in the water. Our University of Texas synchronized swim team went to the national swim meet and placed third. At one of our swim practices, a poster about a dive course caught my attention. That was it: my future was sealed at that moment.

The instructors, Jim Fuller, Paul Johnston, Peter Oliver, Stephanie Scott, and Jim Bowden, were *so* into the sport and so *good* at it that as soon as one course was over, students would run back to the dive shop to sign up for the next one. This was a NAUI (National Association of Underwater Instructors) shop—very detailed and very thorough. From 1980 until 1982 I took every course I could and racked up 250 dives in two years—while going to school full time! My dive partner, Danny Self, and I did research on the lake, salvage under the marinas ... just about any excuse would get us in the water. We once located a university football ring that a man had dropped into the water by the dock. Since we'd spent some time there, we knew what time of year he had lost the ring and figured out where the floating dock would probably have been, allowing for lake-level changes due to drought or excessive rain. We went under, and five minutes later handed him the ring. The look on his face was worth it.

After I received my degree in music education/piano, my parents hoped I would settle down. My dad had taught all his life—high school principal, supervisor of student teachers in South Texas, and education at Texas A&I for years, until he retired. He said the school systems would cover my retirement. My response to him was "What if I die in a car wreck tomorrow?"

My heart said to follow my dream, whatever it was ... and at that time, in 1982, I already wanted to go live on an island. I believe things come our way if we are open to them. I taught scuba diving in Texas from 1982 to 1985, and luck came my way. I had taught some women to dive, and we went to Cozumel. We chartered a boat, did our training dives, and had a *great* time. A couple of years later, they called again and asked if I would go with them to Grand Cayman. Since I had never been there, I suggested local divemasters who knew the reef, but they wanted me along also. So for two weeks, Bitsy Henderson, Laura Robinson, and I dove in Grand Cayman and stayed at a small, quaint resort, South Cove (now replaced by Coconut Harbor). I can still remember hanging onto the stationary mooring line under the boat, surrounded by blue water, and thinking *Hmmm ... I think I could do this for a while.* As soon as I got home my stuff went into storage, and I thanked Bitsy and Laura profusely and moved down to Grand Cayman in 1985. This book is being written in 2003, some eighteen years later—so obviously, I fell in love with the Islands.

But back to Texas. ... My original dive instructor was Jim Fuller, a huge, burly, ex-military teddy bear. He had such enthusiasm for diving and the details of the sport that I was immediately hooked. I couldn't wait for the next lake trip or class. When we first became instructors, we would all go to the lake and set up a secure line with a buoy and dive flag on top, one instructor next to the other. It was all in a safe, protected teaching cove or inlet. Jim would oversee, coordinating instructors, buoys, and students. If the silty bottom got stirred up, the lake visibility would be nil—two feet. We would joke with each other about how many students we needed to bring out of the water. There could easily be some swapping going on down there, but as long as we came back with the correct number, we could sort them out later!

Once we had gone diving, we would usually see Jim F. snorkel down and observe the class while on a breath-hold at around thirty to forty feet. After satisfying himself that my students and I were okay, he would go on to the next buoy and instructor. Susan,[17] a new instructor who was not as strong as some of us, had a nervous student. She would check on the student, move on, and then return to make sure no one had left her class. As I mentioned, lake visibility could deteriorate with a couple of fin scuffles by new divers. At one point, Susan observed fins heading for the surface. She hurriedly grabbed the fins and attempted to keep the student from bolting. The harder the runaway diver kicked, the more Susan was determined to stop this uncontrolled ascent. Susan was eventually dragged all the way up, and the "student" turned out to be Jim F. on a breath-hold dive, observing her class! Needless to say, she earned new respect that day.

Karen Hohle, one of my best girlfriends, reminded

me of a funny story. We met in the dive classes around
the lake and hung out with the same group of divers and
friends. Twenty years later, she would come to Pirates
Point to help out as a Caribbean divemaster if and when
we were shorthanded. Back in Texas, though, one hot
summer day, she was taking her advanced course and
doing triangles and squares underwater. The instructor
had tied Clorox bottles to the students so he could see
their progress from the beach. He wasn't violating safety
rules because there were other dive instructors in the
water, kicking along with the students doing the underwater shapes. There was another dive shop across the
lake whose instructor *did* sit in a chair on the shore. He
was heard to say, "When you come back, we'll discuss
any problems you had." Scary! I had even met some of
his students—when they re-took the dive course with us!

At the lake, each dive shop had its own section staked
out. There were catfish, perch, underwater grottoes and
overhangs, and low visibility. We learned to create our
own fun—by invading the rival shop's area. Each of us
had put a boat or car in our training coves so the students
would have something to look at; plus, over time, the
fish would make it their home. Now, to "steal" a car from
underwater actually takes a lot of work. Four of us went
at night, by boat, slid over the side and into the water,
with lift bags and extra air tanks and rope. After securing
everything, we filled the lift bags at the same time and
cautiously brought the car to the surface. Towing it behind
the boat, we felt a bit like we were in a *Mission: Impossible*
scene. Would spotlights and policemen be on *our* side
of the lake? We drove quietly into our cove, got back into
the water, and gently released the air from the bags to

lower the car to the bottom in about forty feet of water. The next day, they *knew* who had it, and, after various threats of very expensive airfills—or *no* airfills at all—we decided to move the car back to their side of the lake. We had our own compressor for air back in town, but town was thirty minutes away. When you need air at the lake, you need air *now*. So, we repeated the lifting/towing exercise to keep the peace. Lake entertainment.

When I moved to the Cayman Islands in 1985 to become a dive instructor, there was no need to find entertainment to encourage the students. Nature provides a beautiful backdrop for students as they learn to adapt their skills in a bigger, better swimming pool—the ocean! Every day the kaleidoscope of fish—the swirling colors of parrotfish, angelfish, and triggerfish are endless. In the four training dives that are required to get your certification card, it can be a bit overwhelming at first. Not only schools of fish but turtles, sharks, rays, barracuda, and many other critters keep our heads swiveling, looking for what's next. We always have to explain to the students that not *all* of their dives will be this outstanding. The Cayman Islands are one of the top five dive locations in the world! Little Cayman is in a class by itself—it has wall dives that start in eighteen to twenty feet of water, volumes and variety of fish, and new species still being found. During the period when Molly the manta ray was visiting Little Cayman, a couple of training dives were disrupted by her six-foot wingspan as she cruised through class.

Before swimming pools came to Little Cayman, pool sessions and introductory sessions for resort students were done in a shallow, protected part of the ocean called the sound. It is just inside a fringe reef paralleling shore, and it has a natural cut in the reef that is a channel for boats to come in and out. One afternoon I was teaching, and the student and I were having a great time going along the reef in two to five feet of water, when all of a sudden I looked over and saw that a hammerhead had decided to check us out! I directed the student's attention to a school of small fish until the shadow was gone. Yikes! People have a thing about sharks anyway, after *Jaws*, but a hammerhead demands respect. The fishermen say she comes into the sound to give birth to her young ones each winter. She has been seen consistently over the years.

I have one memory of resort students on a dive in Grand Cayman, where I almost drowned laughing. We had pulled up to a famous dive site called Waldo's Reef. There were a couple of resident green eels at home here. As we were attaching to the mooring, I observed something a bit unusual just under the surface, but could not tell what it was ... we'll find out soon enough. After entering, my "resorts" did a great job of following me along the reef. We were halfway into the dive when the unusual critter showed up—trying to attach itself, over and over, to one of my students! It was a *large* remora without a host (shark or ray), trying to find one! Of course, I tried to keep the students' eyes focused on me, but I was laughing so hard at the remora's antics that I was amazed they never realized what was happening. The dive was completed without complications—thank goodness.

Sometimes the dive goes fine, and the complications come afterward. Two couples, the Kahns and Wynnes, come every year and we have great dives and fun. Robert had just boarded the boat—and, within moments, we were all searching the deck for a lost contact lens. No luck. I heard a splash, and looked up to see him with a mask on, paddling about. He always likes to snorkel in the surface interval. However, this time, his wife and friends were chuckling. I had to ask, "What's he doing?" "Looking for his contact!" Clear contact, wall drop-off— I doubt it.

Another resort course brought laughter to my life. I always like to find out a bit about people because we meet all walks of life here. Well, Mark[18] was a professional ballet dancer. As we got to the wall drop-off in Little Cayman, he could contain himself no longer. He did a broad leap and a pirouette as he went over the edge of the wall. It would have been normal on stage, but in full scuba gear, the picture was hilarious.

On the topic of how we look down below—I have a story regarding nudism, which is *against the law* in the Cayman Islands. Neil, our policeman, clarified Cayman's stance on nudism: it is considered "idle and disorderly", and is an arrestable offence if committed in a public place. In fact, since the Islands are a bit prim and proper, it is best to dress appropriately in town, if you want to endear yourself to the locals—for instance, skimpy bathing suits garner disapproving looks. If you don't care what the locals think, wear, or don't wear, what you want.

Around 1990, another Little Cayman resort had asked for my assistance in certifying some of their guests. At that time they didn't have a dive instructor on staff. We arranged that they would pick me up so I could go on their boat. The truck arrived and I piled in with ten divers from Colorado. They seemed like a nice group. We got on the boat, and, all of a sudden, T-shirts were coming off (normal), shorts were dropping (abnormal), and pretty soon I was the only one wearing any clothes! I had no idea it was a *nudist* group! I believe that, as their clothes dropped, my *jaw* dropped. Now, honestly, where do you look, as you brief your stark naked students? Good thing I was taught about eye contact when teaching, because the PADI instructor manual doesn't have a nude-diving specialty ... yet. I briefed them on the skills to do, buddy systems, proper descents and ascents, hand signals, etc., and the only thing I can remember about the talk now is the puffiness of the clouds, the texture of the boat deck, the colors of their hair ... It wasn't until we got in the water that I realized I was staring at their body parts, out of sheer curiosity. *Be careful how close you come to the reef!* It gave a new meaning to having good buoyancy control. *Avoid that fire coral. Tuck everything in so you don't drag the reef!* The funniest part was that, wherever we went that day, my husband, Ed, who had Pirates Point's divers, just "happened" to be doing the dive next to us. He, of course, had heard about the nudist colony on the island-information hotline, the "coconut telegraph". New sightings for logbooks!

Divers wear lead weight to get us under the surface of the water. The amount we use depends on our body composition, type of wetsuit, comfort level, and—most important—our breathing. Any of us who have done diving for a while have learned that most people dive too heavy. I've learned to love doing buoyancy work with people, because it results in less damage to the reef and actually makes them safer divers. We even have one-pound weights to fine-tune. Weights come in one- to six-pound increments. As people become more comfortable in the water, in general, they need less weight to dive.

One September, out we went with Don and Harriet.[19] We had been working with them on shedding some of the weight off their belts, but they took it one step further. One day, Harriet was at the dive platform and asked her husband for another small weight. He walked to his dive bag, pulled out a baggie of various tire-balancing weights, and handed her the necessary ounce. I thought *I* was particular—that is extreme!

Another "weight" story involved a boat sinking. One of the dive boats had gone out, chosen a dive site, and put divers in the water—just like every other day. But this day, as the divers were coming up, the boat was sinking. The next day, we took their divers with us. On the surface interval, we were hearing the story of the sinking boat from the perspective of a new diver. He had just gotten certified in Grand Cayman, and this was his first dive after classes. He said, "I thought I was overweighted in the water, and when I started boarding the ladder and it was sinking to meet me, I KNEW I was overweighted!"

One of my training dives involved a young student. Twelve years old used to be the certifying age, but it has now changed to ten. We joke that someday there will be "infant diving". I had gone over the required hand signals with John.[20] As we started down the rope, I gave him a "stop" signal, palm facing him. He excitedly slapped my palm in a "high five" fashion. We're all learning new hand signals every day—I learned from him.

One form of dive training that we do a lot of is called an open water referral. The person completes pool and classwork back home and, instead of going to a cold, murky lake, comes to the Caribbean to do the certification dives. I had interviewed a couple to see if there were any concerns before we got involved in the water work. The couple assured me they were comfortable and ready to dive. However, on our descent, one thing became very apparent—it is difficult to go down holding a mooring line while clearing your ears AND trying to hold your toupee in place. In fact, at some point, Joe[21] decided his toupee was more important than his dive, so we returned to the boat and I gave him a hood to keep his hair in place. His wife, Jane,[22] had trouble sinking. Usually this is caused by overinflating the lungs in the excitement of the first dives; in Jane's case, she had recently altered her bustline so much that it took quite a few extra pounds to get her underwater. And since she was proud to show off her new, improved bosom, it was interesting watching how buoyant these boobs became, especially on the ascent line. I have now seen people come up feet first, butt first, and boobs first!

Another ascent story comes from my friend Kelly, in Grand Cayman. On all ascents in diving, a safety stop at around fifteen to twenty feet is strongly suggested, to decompress and get rid of some of the nitrogen your body absorbs during the dive. Kelly was quizzing her dive class about these safety procedures. "What do you do at the end of every dive?" she asked. A fourteen-year-old boy, proud of knowing the answer, responded, "On your way up ...", thinking hard, ". . . you stop at fifteen feet for three minutes to decompose!"

Stingray City

Although this book pertains primarily to Little Cayman, I felt one could hardly mention the Cayman Islands without saying something about Stingray City. In fact, a lot of our guests visit the rays, either enroute to Little Cayman or after leaving Pirates Point. If you have read the first part of the book, you know I am not a fan of altered feeding—but the book *is* about humor. When you combine groups of hungry rays with food-totin' tourists, there are bound to be some funny events.

The origins of Stingray City go back to the early days when local fishermen returned to the North Sound with their daily catch. They would come just inside the fringe reef and anchor, then clean the fish and conch and toss the scraps overboard. As this pattern recurred over and over, the southern stingrays (*Dasyatis americana*) figured out that fishing skiffs meant a free meal. As legend has it, early in 1986, the rays became apparent to Pat Kenney and Jay Ireland, dive instructors and boat captains who ran daily drive trips to the North Wall. Between dives, they would bring the boat inside the fringe reef, and they soon discovered that the rays were consistently interested in interaction. Pat, enchanted with the rays' distinct personalities, began to hand-feed and stroke them. He says in the beginning there were three rays—"Hooray", "X-ray", and "Jay-ray"—and then ten, and eventually twenty different rays that they could identify. The first contact with the rays took *a lot* of patience, because they were so shy ... Pat believes they eventually came around because Jay Ireland would put on scuba and spend time with them.

As a tourist, it is best to leave the feeding of the rays up to the professionals. Remember, they've spent *hours* with the creatures. If you *do* want to feed them, please listen *carefully* to the advice of the dive guides. Even then, some people walk away with a souvenir "hickey", produced as the ray lovingly sucks your hand or arm, looking for a treat.

The feeding phenomenon occurs in only twelve feet of water, so it's great for snorkelers as well as scuba divers. It has been nicknamed "The World's Best 12-foot Dive" by *Skin Diver* magazine, "Ballet with Rays" by *National Geographic*, and "It's a Stingray Party" by *Diver* magazine. Jumping into a group of twenty or more southern rays gliding, swooping, sucking, rubbing, and doing all kinds of acrobatics for a tidbit is definitely a great way to spend an hour in nature.

As the boat engines rev, the action begins. Now, remember, these are still wild creatures, and this is not "normal" behavior. Anything can happen. My friend Reid says, "Every day something funny happens." The rays are fed ballyhoo and squid in a "controlled manner".

Here are some stories from "old timers".

As told by Pat Kenney: "When Jay and I first started working with the rays, it was only normal to start naming them, as each one had its own personality and identification. Thus, the names Jay-ray, X-ray, Gamma Ray, Ron-ray, along with a long list of personal names. The only problem was that it was pointed out to us that all the rays that we had given male names to were, in fact, females! We never changed the names, but we did undertake to make ourselves more educated about the stingrays."

A feeding procedure was established, early on, that would put the divemaster on the sand, in the center of a circle of divers. Ballyhoo, a bait fish, is cut in small sections and then fed to the rays, to the delight of the onlookers. Pat had been doing this for quite some time and decided to try an new way to feed them. He describes it as a "very unusual and intimate encounter". Instead of feeding by hand, he put the ballyhoo tail section in his mouth. The rays caught on quickly and would gently inhale the bait from Pat's lips—at least that was the *usual* plan! On one particular occasion, the ray inhaled so strongly that it included Pat's bottom lip! Much to his surprise and shock, the ray did not want to let go of the free food, so it gave a couple of gentle flaps of its large wings and actually lifted Pat off the sandy bottom and carried him ten or fifteen feet—by his bottom lip! At that point, Pat had surpassed what the divers were expecting. What a magnificent stunt! Back at the boat, the response was incredible: "How did you get the ray to *do* that? Way cool! Wow!" Pat says, "Not wanting anyone to think I was uncool, I tried to explain, with my lower lip now swelling to the size of a truck-tire inner tube and impeding my speech more by the second, just how gentle these rays are. A memory I will never forget! Needless to say, it was even harder to explain to my wife when I got home at the end of the day."

After doing the stingray trips for quite some time and having become bored with it, Joe[23] decided to make his own "city". He formed a circle of conch, put a bit of air under each shell, and proceeded to make underwater music. As he gently lifted each shell off the sand bottom, a loud, fart-like sound was emitted. Each shell had a different tone! Pat and Joe, having that perverted dive-master sense of humor, almost drowned laughing underwater that day. "Joe's Conch City"! Not very popular with tourists, but funny to the guides.

It is inevitable that people will feed fish on their own—in fact, in Grand Cayman, canned Cheez Whiz must sell by the case! People squeeze the Cheez Whiz can and are immediately surrounded by hungry fish ... *imagine* our surprise to turn around one day to see someone trying to get a *conch* interested in canned cheese!

One trip included a very petite young Japanese woman. She had put her squid (bait) in her pocket and then put her long black hair in a bun on top of her head. Needless to say, the rays were attracted to her by smell and actually gently sucked onto her head and started bouncing her 95-pound body out of the circle of divers. The divemaster said his mask was flooding as he laughed, but he could see that she was okay.

We had a situation in Little Cayman, after a family had been to Stingray City. The next day on the boat, there was a horrible smell from someone's gear. We suggested that all the guests wash their suits, etc. The next day the smell was even worse, almost unbearable, as the summer heat "cooked" something. We *finally* found some dead squid—stingray bait—in the young kid's dive gear—he'd forgotten that he had it!

Sue Barnes and Kirsten, who dive with us a lot, had some funny images from this twelve-foot dive. One was "the altered diver"—doing underwater yoga and something akin to the moonwalk. They also remembered seeing a red wetsuit and Santa hat entertaining the rays and guests around Christmastime one year.

- Do they sell shirts at Stingray City?
- Are the rays pets?
- Is there a phone booth at Stingray City?
- Is there shopping there?

One divemaster, Scotty S., remembers getting ready to jump in just behind the guests when a woman asked, "What's that big fish?" Nonchalantly, he reassured her that it was nothing to be concerned with ... she insisted the fish was as big as she was. "Yeah, right," thought Scotty, when he suddenly realized he was seeing the shadow of a hammerhead cruising around this lady. In record time, the boat was re-boarded.

Along with the funny stories, there are fishermen's tales of rays coming to fishermen and divemasters for help. I've heard many times of rays sitting calmly while a fishhook or net was cut loose to allow the ray freedom again. A bonding in nature is possible. Even though we do not alter by feeding in Little Cayman, we have had phenomenal experiences with the underwater world. My mind starts to question ...

- *Does the baby ray learn from his mom to come to Stingray City for food?*
- *Do the rays eat anything but prepared food anymore?*
- *Are the rays being overfed as the volume of boats and people increases?*
- *Could the rays go back to surviving without Stingray City?*

There are now guidelines for "doing" Stingray City. Many places around the world have tried to re-create such a unique attraction. It is found only in the Cayman Islands—and worth the trip. The guidelines include:

- Restrict feeding to the appointed tour operator.
- Use fish and squid, rather than manufactured food, when feeding the rays.
- Limit the amount of food fed to the stingrays.

- Ensure that any uneaten food and litter are retrieved.
- Always wear gloves when interacting with the rays.

These guidelines have been added because nowadays there can be fifteen to twenty boats, sometimes twice a day, visiting Stingray City. Pat Kenney, who gave me the history of Stingray City as he and Jay found it in the early 1980s, says it is in a critical stage now, twenty years later.

The sandbar is another ray feeding site—originally a place where the people who lived on Grand Cayman would go on their days off. It is shallower than Stingray City, and Pat says it has grown from ten to fifteen rays to more than sixty resident rays. He says the rays are increasing at an alarming rate and that the females are some of the largest rays around.

Even after discussing the pros and cons of this tourist attraction, his final comment was that the positive impact greatly outweighed the negative. The following story, told by Pat Kenney, attests to that.

"I was captaining the *Spirit of Ppalu* catamaran. There were fifty customers on board for a snorkel trip to Stingray City ... a very nice trip, I might add. Once at Stingray City, they were given a briefing and entered the water. I had slipped in off the stern on scuba and had begun to feed the rays. I would feed them and gently coax them to the surface, and the customers would stroke and pet them.

"Many of these people had only viewed these beautiful creatures as evil/dangerous. However, once they interacted with them they fell in love with them and took a much different attitude toward the rays and the sea ... much more careful and respectful. Anyway, during this feeding, a nice blacktip shark showed up ... about five or six feet long. I looked up and expected to see this sea of snorkelers walking on water and crawling over each other to get back on board the boat.

"Not so; they were mesmerized, and just floated on the surface enjoying the show. I slowly made my way back to the surface ... remembering I was carrying a large baggie full of chopped bait, and being eyed by the visiting shark.

"As I got to the surface and prepared to have the customers return to the boat, several customers stopped me and asked, 'When are you going to hand-feed the shark?' Needless to say, I was shocked, and then realized that only a few years ago, after the movie *Jaws*, people had developed an intense fear of sharks. But these people, after being properly briefed and interacting with the stingrays, seemed to take a more positive, caring attitude toward not only the rays but the shark as well."

So, if you are planning a trip to Stingray City, please keep the guidelines in the back of your mind ... so that this attraction can be around for *your* children, too.

9

Things aren't always what they seem ...

I chose this title because so often in life, not just on islands, we look at someone or something and assume *Aha! I know what happened!* Yet it may not necessarily be true. Some such events occur naturally, and some are set up as pranks. You get a bit of both in this chapter.

Often an island destination will advertise something that is not quite what really is ... so read between the lines. The one I love is the difference between "oceanfront" and "oceanview". They may seem similar but are *very* different. *Oceanfront* describes the room where you see the ocean from your bed, whereas *oceanview* means you leave the bed, lean out the door as far as you can, and then around the corner is the ocean.

We heard rumors that oil had been struck on the middle island, Cayman Brac. The true story was a bit different: a machine was digging a hole and a hydraulic oil hose severed, causing oil to start spewing skyward, giving false hopes of fortune.

Gladys had stopped to buy groceries in Grand Cayman on her way back here. She was approached in the parking lot by a woman who asked her to buy some raffle tickets. She came home, excited, with multiple tickets and chances of possibly winning a car. I asked her when the drawing was to be held. As she read the drawing date off the ticket, her face fell—the drawing had been two weeks ago. But we did get a laugh, thinking of that lady in the parking lot, skipping away with the money. We hoped she got what she needed from the sale of those *old* raffle tickets.

Art Gale, who used to be a mechanic in Little Cayman, tells the story of a traffic jam in Grand Cayman, but not for the normal fender-bender reasons. A cow was tied to a pickup, and the inconsiderate driver was allowing it a comfortable amble during rush hour! Obviously, there was no "rush" involved on anyone's part.

One day Ed and I were driving to the dive boat. We passed the new church and, out of the corner of my eye, I saw a guy standing there with a *huge* arc of water coming from his pants. I was *amazed* that he could pee that far—then realized it was the way he was holding the garden hose. Now, a quick glance, without seeing the hose, could have given rise to quite a rumor about the gardener!

Maybe it's island life, or maybe it's because I'm getting older, but humor seems to have become more and more an essential part of my day. And it derives from the simplest things. I used to be so serious, so intent, that I missed a lot of the smaller things. I believe that most people are this way. One of my main goals in life now is to see the humor and the lesson in any event.

One deceptive area of island life is romance. Someone once asked me, in all sincerity, "Do you have the same moon we have back home?" Unbelievable! Wow! How do people survive the day-to-day world? I realize they relax on vacation—but some of this stuff is scary!

People traveling to islands find themselves in some spectacular romantic settings, which can do wonders for a relationship. That same romantic setting can lure people into believing they are in a really great relationship—but would the same relationship survive back home? It's fascinating to watch. A lot of island workers pair up, but could you see them going home to meet the parents? ... maybe not. A lot of people who live on islands are a bit detached. They enjoy the comings and goings of guests because it's great fun—but not too close.

I like observing people. In fact, as a dive instructor, your observations about people can become the key to your success. Listening, caring, being helpful, sometimes being a bit stern ... Each person or situation is different and needs to be treated as such. Some friends of mine observed Bruce,[24] who had a girl visiting from the States. They had had a great week. When they were at the airport, she gave him one last hug and tearfully asked when they would see each other again. We imagined he used the island saying "Soon come". As soon as she walked away, he turned and headed toward the incoming planes to pick up the next girlfriend! She had inadvertently picked an arrival date a *little* too close to the departure date of her predecessor. This is not the norm, but it *is* funny.

Speaking of romance, John and Marilyn Palmer, who own a house right across from Owen Island, said I could write a whole book on honeymooners who come to the islands. In fact, THEY could write a book, from all their observations over the years! It's easy to imagine that on Owen Island, people assume that they're hidden from view, when, in actuality ... they *are* the view. The tiny, uninhabited island is in the middle of the sound, and though the beach faces the Southern Cross Club and private homes, it feels totally private. The Palmers have some hilarious stories of honeymooners swimming nude, consummating their love for each other on the beach and in the water ... you get the idea. The funniest time was when the Palmers heard thrashing and screams and thought someone might be drowning or in need of help

... nope, we're just fine here. Imagine! What if this were *your* front yard?! The joys of being a homeowner in the Caribbean ...

Some events are not laughing matters at all—but sometimes, in the islands, the story can get twisted as someone sees or hears only part of it, and the result can't help but be funny.

An elderly lady named Helen[25] had been coming to Little Cayman for a number of years to study termites, sponsored by the Smithsonian Institution. Each year she would walk the island's bush and beaches, looking for evidence of termites and how they got here. She carried a shovel, a burlap bag full of bottles to contain the different types of termites, and a huge sun hat. She would disappear for hours on end. Every time she returned from hunting, she would be as excited as a kid and would prattle on and on about this type, that one, etc. I could not get excited about termites, but I *could* appreciate the twinkle in her eye and her obsession. (Mine just happens to be with seahorses.) Anyway, after a busy morning with the bugs, she would always take a nap—sitting up. In fact, when she stayed with us, we gave her a wicker chair that had a slope to it, so she could sleep comfortably in this position. After napping, she would be off and running again—more logs to turn, more termites to see!

She had traced the termites to logs that were floating to our beaches, and, knowing the tree, deduced that most of our termites were coming from Jamaica. One year, she went to Jamaica to try to find out what was happening on that end, hoping to stop the arrival of the termite logs. I can just see her waving a machete among the locals.

Over the years, Helen had stayed at all the resorts, so the sight of her napping, sitting up, had become commonplace. One day, as the colors in the sky began to change and happy hour was around the corner, people became aware that she had napped a bit longer than usual. Someone went to wake her up, but she had died peacefully during her nap!

Now, what to do ... they took her to her room and made all the necessary phone calls. Don't get me wrong here—death isn't funny—but not everyone knew she was dead yet. And for the next couple of hours, various men were seen coming and going from her room. You can imagine the stories circulating!

Gladys, Pirates Point's owner, is always ready for a birthday, holiday, or party, and goes all out to have fun. In fact, her daughter, Susan, gave her a funny hat one Christmas that features a pig's head and says "Party Animal". Gladys created a Mardi Gras parade in Little Cayman (more on this later) that has become an annual event, growing every year, in which the resorts and residents enter elaborate floats with themes, all hoping to win prizes for best float, best costume, etc. Gladys takes it seriously. She *loves* to win—and deserves to, because of her attention to detail and her dedication to making the float accurate and true to the theme. (As of this writing, we have a five-year winning streak. I hope I'm not jinxing it by sharing this with you!)

One day, Gladys was watching an *Alice in Wonderland* video, taking notes. She was pausing the tape, rewinding, fast forwarding, and obviously studying, while jotting down information. You'd have thought there was going to be a written exam the next day, she was so engrossed in her project. The float would represent Alice in Wonderland perfectly. The same morning, Martha was interviewing one of our new divers. We give them an orientation talk, tell them about our style of diving, and find out a bit about their diving background before going in the water with them. He was listening to the briefing, but he kept leaning back and glancing over at Gladys, fascinated with her attention to the video. Finally he asked, "Is she taking notes?" Martha, who had seen this *many* times before, responded, "Yes", but continued on with the dive orientation, never missing a beat. (*No, the owner is not watching cartoons.*)

Since this chapter is about things not always being what they seem, I thought island pranks would fit in well. In the earlier years, just about anyone who lived here had that twinkle-in-the-eye sense of humor. You had to—it was essential for living here. But Tom Hernandez and John and B.J. Mulak were the undisputed geniuses behind quite a few of Little Cayman's memorable pranks—not to discount anyone else ... Back then, there were no rules, no regulations, no street lights, no policemen ... there was no *need* for regimentation. More people, more rules.

Remote island ... pirate history ... treasure. I think this thought passed through everyone's mind when we all first came here. Apparently, though, anything found is supposed to be turned in to the government or the National Museum. Colored bottles, pieces of china, coins, cannons, and cannonballs have all been found here. One area where cannons were found came complete with coins! I know a load of coins were taken out to the States by private plane, and the next thing we knew, signs were posted at the site and the airport warning of jail sentences for anyone caught taking anything from the historic site. It kept me away! But the funny searches usually involved a bit of a set-up. Some pirates[26] had gone searching for treasure. There are some older, defunct homesteads back in the bush, which seemed promising for loot. The north coast of the island has always been the last part of this island to be looked at ... so it seemed to make sense to look there. Metal detectors were smelling the ground and beeping frequently. The group thought they had hit paydirt. The coins kept rolling in—wow! But it turned out they were American pennies ... 1989 seemed to be the oldest. Funny—that's the year Tom came here.

As I said, north coast gets everything last. Since the breeze comes predominantly from the south, most resorts and homes face that direction. But the people who live north *like* being out there by themselves. We all viewed development in more or less the same way: the less, the better. Of course it is nice having amenities, but ... Anyway, the north coast people usually come for months at a time, up to half or even most of the year. After having been gone for a while, they returned to find a new feature for guests cycling around the island—a port-a-potty. It sat right on the boundary line of someone's property. It came complete with pipe out the side, balls of mud nearby, and toilet paper available—trailing over the toilet seat. The crowning touch was a sign that read PUBLIC RESTROOM 1/4 MILE. That one got a lot of chuckles.

To carry the joke one step further, a fake form was mailed from the Department of Lands and Survey stating that the property had been resurveyed and that fifteen feet was being taken away to be used as a public beach access. This is why the outhouse was made available—joke complete with colored tape leading to the water!

Another prank involved the change from generators to electricity. The days of going home and starting up your own generator were coming to an end—and north coast was last to come on line with central power. They had been waiting quite a while. A sign was posted, by "a friend", on the telephone pole, about twenty feet high, so it couldn't be knocked down:

> Dear Brac Power—do not put a transformer here—we do not want electricity. We have a very good generator that runs well. When it fails, we will contact you ...

This one almost backfired. Eventually, Tom[27] had to tell the power company it was a joke. They weren't going to take power out that far. Oops!

At one point, Gladys, who has for many years chaired the Little Cayman committee of the National Trust, was trying to persuade people to donate small pieces of land around the Booby Pond. These were not the primary lots that their homes were built on but pieces across the paved road from the house lots—a tiny strip of land that most people did not want to give away. One resident received a letter that looked pretty legitimate, stating that his land would be converted into a government storage area for the fleet of trucks (garbage truck, mosquito spray truck, etc.) and maintenance area. The joke was allowed to sink in until it was rumored that Joe[28] was going to make some inquiring phone calls on Monday. Then the prankster stepped forward and stopped the joke—just in time!

Sometimes the joke is unending. I might be giving this one away—but no names! I will just say that there are *no* monkeys on Little Cayman. There have been some "heard" throughout the year, even in rainstorms, but no actual sightings have occurred. Enough said—use your imagination.

Sometimes the gag is a distracting noise. One truck got rigged with a smoke detector under the front seat that made a low-battery chirping sound—whether the engine was running or not! The frustrated owner was ready to unhook the truck battery to stop the noise, but even that would not have stopped the incessant beeping.

Another fun one involved a house alarm bell alternating with a police siren (this was before the days of the policeman living here). It was hidden in the seagrape trees and would come on about every three to five minutes. The homeowners' first thought was "It's got to be Hernandez." As the story is handed down, when they came to the door to look for the source of the noise, they were less than fully clothed. This was a surprise for Tom, hiding in the bushes. Maybe he should try this at each house! "Peeping Tom" ...

Some pranks consist of an item that gets passed around within the joke circle. The heavily perfumed red negligee was stuffed under beds and between car seats—and came in between some relationships. It was given to a happily married couple, a jealous couple, and a troubled couple—each of which had a different response. The happy couple passed it on. The jealous couple *pretended* they were breaking up and that she was moving out of the house because she found the negligee—which was not true. When told it was a joke, she replied, "It's too late!" Of course, they got the prankster good. As they left the store one day, they threw the negligee into the truck belonging to the troubled couple. The wife of the cheating husband thought he was making it up to her with the nightie!

Another item that got passed around a lot—which would have looked great in the negligee—was a pair of mannequin legs. The legs went everywhere! Upside down in trees, stuck in trash cans, in a toilet bowl inside a gazebo, sticking out of car windows, standing up in the sand beside a bar ... They would be stolen for a while and then reappear. Some of the funniest places they showed up:

- Stuck in a toilet bowl at the end of someone's dock, with a sign that said "For Pete's[29] sake".
- Under a porch. At first glance someone thought it was a drunk from the night before!
- Floating in the road after a heavy rainstorm.

We're not really sure where the legs are now, but I'm sure they're still on the island, waiting to be used again.

Some people make signs to create a joke. There was a "Dr. Kevorkian" sign posted near a retired surgeon's home for a while. Fortunately, he has a great sense of humor! Another sign was placed outside of Pirates Point, but we had no idea it was there. We kept getting outside visitors requesting bike tours. We get a lot of outside dinner guests, but bike tours? We don't even do those for inhouse guests! We finally decided to go out by the roadside and see what was luring people up the driveway. An old, decrepit bike had been placed on the farthest, unused corner of the front lawn. A sign was posted next to it, reading "For bike tours, check within ..."

Another sign, outside the home of an expat who had a lot of bicycles in various stages of disrepair, said "Bicycle repair shop—repairs/rentals/sales". Apparently this was meant to be funny, but it backfired and upset some people. To live and work here, you must do a job that no Caymanians are available to do. A "local" could well have a bike repair shop, so the Caymanians weren't happy to see this particular sign.

One north side prankster told tourists to go to the house next door, where they served great lunches. The tourists were told "There's no sign, but just go in and wait; someone will be right with you." Imagine the homeowners' shock to find two strangers sitting quietly at the dining table, waiting for lunch service!

HALLOWEEN

Tom and Dianne Hernandez were known for showing up each year for Halloween with *the* winning costumes. Pirates Point holds one of the best Halloween parties in the Islands, and there are some unique outfits—but Tom always won first prize. One year he was carried to the party in a full-size coffin. The lid was raised, and, as Dracula, he lay there for half of the party! The next year he was carried in, wearing a straitjacket. His death sentence was announced, and then his pals threw a rope over a tree and hanged him. It looked real! He had built a harness inside the straitjacket to support his body weight. The last party at which I remember seeing him, we had to wait ... we were halfway through the party, and I had just asked if anyone had seen Tom. All of a sudden, the sound of a chainsaw was heard, people started moving to the sides of the room, and Tom came in, carrying a chainsaw and a human-size doll leg that was dripping "blood". Fresh kill.

On Halloween things are *never* what they seem. The fishnet stockings, high-heeled pumps, and short, flashy skirt topped by a well-filled low-cut top may not belong to the new girl in town. A lot of the male divemasters convincingly transform themselves for one night, to see what being in high heels is all about (a lot of work!). They get a little help with their makeup. I have actually seen guys do a double take as a female impersonator walked seductively through the party. Flaunt it!

Pirates Point has been hosting the Halloween party for years, and it has turned into one of the best parties on all three islands. In fact, each island is usually represented by some costumed people—M&Ms, a nurse, an octopus, a flashily dressed tourist complete with camera and set of *bad* fake teeth, aliens, headless people, and various others. Southern Cross Club inevitably has the best staff group appearance. One year they stormed the dance floor in kilts, to the theme from *Braveheart*. Another year they came accurately disguised as the *Star Wars* characters. It's an event worth attending just for the costumes.

At one of these memorable parties, Gladys's truck disappeared. Two of the staff members went off to find it and found a guy who lives on Cayman Brac, driving the truck by the airport. They pulled him over and asked, "What are you doing with our truck?" He drunkenly mumbled, "I'm going home!" Apparently, he was too drunk to remember that "home" was on another island, separated from us by open ocean!

As you can tell by now, Gladys likes costumes and

parties. The annual Mardi Gras party and parade that she started in 1993 has a different theme each year, picked by the Little Cayman National Trust Committee. The community also chooses a person or a couple each year to be honored for their contributions to the island. Once the theme is chosen, resorts and residents build their floats. Over the years, we have created two costume closets at the resort to house all the outfits designed for the parade. Gladys can be seen busily sewing and creating each year, and Pirates Point has had a well-deserved winning streak for best float. The parade is complete with costumed entrants throwing beads to the "crowd". ("Crowd" normally connotes people lining the streets, elbow to elbow, many people deep. Our "crowds" are anywhere from five to fifteen people standing in front of the resorts watching the parade go by—but they make up for their small numbers in enthusiasm!)

I want to recognize the people who have been chosen to be King or Queen of Little Cayman over the years, and have listed them by year with the theme of the parade.

1993	Gladys B. Howard	Mardi Gras
1994	Ray & Betty van Cullen	Underwater
1995	Jack & Rilly Ebanks	Fantasea Island
1996	Brigitte Kassa	Birds
1997	Jeff Smith	King of Hearts
1998	John & B.J. Mulak	Circus
1999	Janet Walker	Hollywood
2000	Peter Hillenbrand	New Orleans
2001	John & Marilyn Palmer	Disney
2002	Betty Bua	Music
2003	Linton & Polly Tibbetts	Cayman Islands Quincentennial

2004   Ed and Gay Morse   Creator's Glory

A couple of costumes that stick out in my mind are from the year we did Circus. The tall man was one of our then chefs, who was six-three; he stood and walked on three-foot stilts hidden under wide-legged pants in a bright clown material. Jerry[30] would reach down and grab the midget's hand, and what a pair they were—the shock on people's faces was priceless. The midget was actually our other chef—who walked the whole parade on his knees! We had converted shoes to fit his knees, and a skirt draped over his legs and trailed behind him. His outfit was completed with a sunbonnet and three-tiered parasol. Quite the couple! Other costumes that year included a strong man with fake five-hundred-pound barbells, a lion and lion tamer with a training whip, a ringmaster with an authentic early-1900s jacket, and many red-nosed, multicolored happy and sad clowns. Circus was probably the favorite theme of all—it was easy and fun to portray the characters.

Ten-Room Resort: Behind the Scenes in Little Cayman

Little Cayman—the most pristine and undeveloped of the three Cayman Islands. There is some history of earlier settlements, but the famous 1932 storm left this island pretty much uninhabited. It is ten miles long by one mile wide. At one time, you would drive to one end of the island and could see the lights of Cayman Brac, just a short distance away. Then you would turn around and go to the other dead end. Now the road goes all the way around the island—however, it is not all paved road. The paving has been done a section at a time. As for power, until 1992 everyone had a diesel generator. The three original resorts were the Southern Cross Club, built as a private fishing camp in the late 1950s; Pirates Point, a home that was turned into a six-room resort and then revamped by Gladys into a ten-room dive resort with gourmet food; and Sam McCoy's Lodge, which is run by a local family and offers Caymanian cuisine with fishing and diving. When there were just three resorts, everyone on the island was pretty much self-contained and self-sufficient—you had to be if you were going to stay for any length of time.

There were only a few homeowners at that time. Little Cayman had no grocery store, no power plant, lots of undeveloped land, no condominiums, and very few people. In fact, the people who lived here then (fifteen full-time residents) could have been contenders on the TV show *Survivor*! The water we had was what fell from the sky, supplemented by the resorts' reverse-osmosis plants (water is taken from the sea, sent through a series of membranes to purify it, and stored in cisterns under the buildings).

The island was all about community. The supply barge was not a consistent service because of mechanical breakdowns and, of course, the weather factor. We learned to share with each other. There was no law enforcement and none needed. It was a good-neighbor policy: "I'll trade you two tomatoes for a cucumber ..." As you can imagine, this quiet, sleepy island, with no street lights, no theft, no locks on the doors, friendly people, very few vehicles, and no noise or light pollution caught on.

Of course, with generators and the unstable supply situation, there were nights when the lights were out by nine o'clock to conserve diesel until the next boat. Sometimes we served dinner by candlelight out of necessity. But when the generators were off, you could *really* appreciate how peaceful and quiet it was.

Improvisation was a part of everyday life. If you needed a part for something, it would "soon come", but until that day came, you learned to make do. Many guests who visited Pirates Point in the early days loved it because it was an adventure and so different from back home. Even now, with the development that occurred after central power came in 1992, Little Cayman still has a wonderful ambience, and the people who have gravitated here to live are what make the place so special. Of course, the guests also make the resort fun. Some of the guests we would like to return straight back to the airport, but since that isn't an option, we get a great opportunity to work on ourselves—patience, tolerance, and *remember-it's-only-a-week*. Actually, we *love* seeing most of our guests over and over—and we do, because we average eighty percent repeat customers. We have been through a life journey with most of them—births, deaths, marriages, divorces, new homes, loss of their home, new puppy, death of an old pet ... you name it. That is what is so neat about a small resort. You *must* like people, though.

In the title to this chapter, I promised to go behind the scenes. Unfortunately, many good stories have faded from memory, and I didn't seriously think of writing this book until a couple of years ago ... but I hope you will get a few laughs, as we did when we remembered these occasions.

Since Pirates Point Resort is all about peace and quiet, great food, diving, and atmosphere, we tend to get a lot of professional people looking to slow down. No TVs or phones in the rooms ... perfect. We can see in their faces that they don't allow themselves a lot of down time. We get hard evidence that a relaxed atmosphere and a fun staff can bring about a total transformation in these guests. This is one of the joys of working in a small resort in the Caribbean. But back to the story ... I had picked up Frank[31] from the airport and taken him to his oceanfront room. His face showed signs of exhaustion from the long hours of traveling—catching the "redeye" in order to make it here in one day, and losing sleep because of the late-night flight. Of course, in the previous week he had probably doubled his usual working hours so he would be caught up enough to leave on this vacation. Sound familiar? The next morning at breakfast, he looked worse to me, so I asked, "How did you sleep? Can we do anything for you?" He replied, "I *couldn't* sleep—the sound of the ocean was like a freight train coming through my room all night!" (Think how many people buy white-noise machines to *hear* the ocean!) I assured him that over the week, he would catch up on his sleep. There are lots of hammocks around the property, and most people find it no problem to drop off for a siesta after a beautiful day of diving and a filling lunch.

As the week went on, Frank was relaxing, catching some rays of sunshine, and losing the fluorescent pallor associated with his job. His last night, at dinner, I asked him how his week had gone. The transformation had occurred, and his face showed it. He replied with a laugh, "About midweek, the sound of the ocean was lulling me to sleep. I slept like a baby." This is why I continue to work in the Caribbean. The connection we get to experience with other people, the sharing of stories, the return visits.

As I've mentioned, most of our guests are repeat visitors. Sometimes, though—it's very rare, but it does happen!—a guest just doesn't fit. The staff notices first, but—believe it or not—our other guests come up and ask us what the problem is with that person ... so we do have a blacklist. We joke about it and tease some of our new guests about not wanting to get on "the list". I've seen people actually take a dinner place setting and move it to a different table, explaining that they had just met this couple and wanted to visit ... and, eventually, the obnoxious person is left at a table alone with his partner. Like I said, it's very rare where we work, but ...

One particular group of seven divers had been ignoring the mandatory 100-foot Cayman depth rule and were dropping off the wall. In the dining room, they would burp and fart. They left a driftwood bar sign that said

"Go Deep or Go Home". Well, you can guess what we told them. We banned them. They *did* want to come back, but we just kept saying we were full, whenever they wanted to come. As it turns out, they have not only been banned from all the resorts on Little Cayman; later on the boat, I heard about them from guests who had seen them banned from Belize and Cozumel! What a reputation!

When people leave, they can pay by personal check, traveler's check, or credit card. One day, a guy who worked at a carnival asked if he could pay with cash—sure thing! Of course, I'm counting hundreds in my mind. When he returned to pay, he gave me *stacks* of five- and ten-dollar bills! At that time, there was no bank in Little Cayman … can you imagine taking the wads of cash into the States?

Then there are people who want to return, but not always with the same person! Joan and Harold[32] had come for a week of diving and obviously enjoyed each other's company. When they were leaving, they vowed to return soon. So about six months later, when Joan called, I asked her if Harold was coming with her. There was a pause, and then she said, "No, this time I'm bringing my husband, Matt. Please don't mention Harold." Well, I wrote in big red letters on her reservation NOT to mention Harold. The day I was going to the airport, I reminded myself not to recognize her. We always hug return guests, and sure enough, I found myself hugging her before remembering she supposedly had never been here before. I mumbled something about "Didn't I dive you in Grand Cayman years ago …?" and she said, "Yeah! I knew I had seen you before!" Great save! He never noticed.

One really nice thing about Little Cayman is the sense

of peace. It's safe, and nobody is begging or accosting you to buy drugs, like on some other islands. In fact, at the resort, we don't even give the guests room keys—there *are* none! Whenever New Yorkers come in, you can tell they're a bit unsure about this unlocked-door policy. They always seem to be looking over their shoulders until later in the week. (We do now have lock boxes in the lobby for people who feel the need to lock up wallets, passports, and other valuables.) I had finally persuaded a couple how safe it is here, so imagine my shock when, the next morning, the lady came in and said, "We have a problem ...". She described how, in the middle of the night, someone came in their front door, quietly walked around, went into the bathroom, brushed their teeth, then walked back out of the room. Of course, Mrs. New York had stayed glued to the bed, thinking it was a thief! There are two oceanfront rooms to a building, so I looked up their duplex neighbors. They were a couple who have been coming here for years. (No names because they still come here. I'm hoping if they read this, they won't remember!) It turned out the woman was sleepwalking. Our remedy was to lock the front door, leaving the ocean-side door open. The New Yorkers could get in and out ... but the sleepwalker never returned.

Another case of mistaken rooms: a couple had come to the resort with a *very* nice pair of binoculars, for birding after diving. They were apparently knowledgeable about birds and loved to study them through the binoculars. After a couple of days, they announced to the group at the resort that they must have misplaced their field glasses. They tried to remember when they had last used them. The way they described it, it all involved their mishandling of the missing glasses. Meanwhile ... a family of four was having a great week. Mom and Dad were diving while the daughter and grandmother were snorkeling and beachcombing. Josephine[33] went to the room to get the family's binoculars for birding one day, only she went to the wrong room. She ended up with very nice pair of binoculars—which weren't hers! Finally someone noticed, and the binoculars were returned, but a little too late for birding that week.

Sometimes it's fun to let your mind play with what *might* have happened. The guest is no longer here to verify or discount the story. Carl and Beth Campbell are some of our original guests—I'm sure I could write a second book featuring all of our repeat guests' memories! One day, they were hanging their bathing suits out to dry and saw an abandoned bathing suit in the bush behind their room. When they turned it in to "lost and found", we had a good laugh putting together scenarios about how the bathing suit ended up there. Use your *own* imagination!

At Pirates Point we are always experiencing neat events with people. The atmosphere promotes a bonding between staff and guests that is unique in my experience. One year, Rodale's scuba magazine ran an article about a man who was eighty-six years old and claimed to be the world's oldest scuba diver. In fact, he was challenging anyone who was older to speak up. Immediately Pirates Point and Southern Cross Club submitted a profile of a *long*time guest of both resorts—Ed Ball. At the time, he was ninety-five years old, dove regularly, and had fifteen hundred logged dives. One challenge he set himself, when he was ninety, was a dive at the Arctic Circle. He

drilled out a circle of ice, jumped in, and got out. Whew—
no thanks! He continued diving until he was ninety-
eight. Was *he* the oldest diver? Who knows?

A unique thing happened one morning as we were
transporting our divers to the resort's dock, which is
about a mile from the resort. As the divers were loading
onto the open truck benches, one of the young men
suddenly said, "Dad, is that you?!" This young guy was
on his honeymoon, and in the next truck over, unbeknownst to him, was his dad! Because of an unsettled
and unhappy past, their relationship had ended on a
sour note—seventeen years before. One of the couples
was leaving the next day, so they had twenty-four hours
to rehash the past and patch up the relationship. Small,
remote, ten-room resort—same week, randomly picked.
What are the chances? It was truly heartwarming to see
them reconnect. I don't know what you believe, but I
think things happen for a reason. People and events are
put in our lives, or back into our lives, and to me, this was
a perfect example.

We play a lot of dominoes at Pirates Point, in the
evenings after dinner. Remember, in Little Cayman you
learn to make your own fun! The island is nature at its
best, but there's no night life. When we're playing dominoes, it can get pretty rowdy. The most fun is a game
called Mexican Train. The rules of the game change,
depending on which guests are here playing. Gladys tends
to be very vocal, whether she's winning or losing, and it
keeps the game hopping along. One night an Irishman
was here, who had *no* idea how engrossing a game of
dominoes could be ... until a couple of hours later, after
a couple of rounds of the game and twice as many beers,

he started betting Gladys. (No betting or gambling is allowed in the Cayman Islands, so I would call this verbal taunting.) He bet his Irish pub against Pirates Point Resort that he would win. Let's just say ... Gladys now owns a pub in Ireland. On one of her trips, she was passing through Ireland, so she stopped in with a huge Texas flag to claim her property. Patrick responded by handing her the bills for re-roofing the bar!

Caymanians SLAM the dominoes down. They play at the same table each night, usually outside under a shade tree, and you can hear them crack the dominoes as the game goes on.

Even though Little Cayman has grown over the years, as of 2003 there are still only a few more than a hundred people on the island. As tourism develops on any island, amenities continue to improve because people want to come on vacation ... but not quite rough it. Although Pirates Point has refrained from putting TVs or phones in the rooms, there is a guest phone in the lobby, along with movies and videos for entertainment. In fact, just this year, the Wynnes and Kahns donated a DVD player and some movies. I rarely see anyone using them. Our hope is that people will see what Little Cayman is all about—nature at its finest: phenomenal wall diving and, on land, great birding.

Earlier in the book, I shared a bunch of tourist questions, mostly from Grand Cayman. As amenities come, the questions have changed ...

- "Is the daily paper here yet?" (*Ha! We get the "daily" about three to five days later!*)
- "Can I get the *New York Times* faxed in daily while I'm there?"

- "Can I borrow a computer to check my stocks today ... and tomorrow ...?"
- "Do you live here?" (*Had to put that one in!*)
- "I work and live in Little Cayman, but I spend the weekends in Grand Cayman. That means I don't pay rent for the weekends, because I'm not there, right?"

We picked up a guest who was having dinner at the resort one evening, and during a five-minute van ride, he discussed the rescheduling of his dinner in Tokyo on his cell phone with his secretary. Then there was the guy who came straight off the boat and hurried to use the phone to make sure his company hadn't folded in his absence.

Yet, I have seen modern conveniences used advantageously. On my breakfast shift one morning, I had just walked in and had to run to answer the phone. It was only 7:00 a.m. I couldn't figure out who would be calling so early. Did they need a reservation? Want to go diving? Who knows? I picked up the phone, only to hear a garbled "... locked ..." *scratch scratch static* "... stuck ...", more static, and then the line went dead! We've had plenty of bad connections on the phone system here. In fact, in the earlier days, it was a radiophone. But this ... hmmm. Okay, back to breakfast prep, only to have the phone ring again. I returned to the phone, a little bit perturbed by now. "Hello, Pirates Point Resort. How can I help you?" The third time, a gentleman clearly said, "We are in room number three and our door is locked! Could you please come let us out of our room?" Then the phone disconnected. I was laughing 'til tears ran down my face. We haven't used keys to lock rooms since Gladys bought the place in 1986. In fact, we don't even *have* room keys. Anyway, I took a screwdriver to go "break in" and let the guests out of their room. As I was relating the story to one of the other staff, they said that it had happened the previous week, but those people hadn't had a cell phone. Someone had walked by their room and seen them plastered against the window, waving and shouting and happy to be released. Needless to say, that particular doorknob got changed in short order!

Another way that modern times has affected Pirates Point is that the resort has been featured in quite a few magazines—*Travel & Leisure, Outside, Gourmet, Bride's Magazine,* and more. In fact, Gladys has never advertised and has created a smashingly successful business through word of mouth alone. When an article comes out, it's great, because it's usually about not only the resort but the personality of the place. One afternoon, Martha was on office duty when she received a call from a woman requesting information. This is an everyday occurrence—however, this lady was in the aisle of a Borders Books, reading Kay Showker's book *100 Best Resorts in the Caribbean.* The only two Cayman Islands resorts mentioned were the Hyatt and Pirates Point. It shows what a long way the resort has progressed since 1986.

Over the years, a few traditions created by Gladys have grown and are worth mentioning because they're so much fun. Early on, the guests started leaving driftwood signs and creations, and Gladys decided to have an art contest each year. The winner gets one free week's package at the resort! We supply the paints, glue guns, nails, and tools, and the guests have to find the other items. It has worked out well, because they go to the beaches and drag home debris and then when they are done, we get rid of the beach trash. Some of the creations appeal to our sense of humor, while others are literally works of art. Nature has been represented by transforming driftwood into a green eel, an authentic-looking heron, a minutely detailed iguana, and a school of fifty different types of fish and sponges in one coral head.

In the humorous category, there is a lifesize rendition of a blond divemaster (me!) with turquoise dive skin and coconuts to represent my rear end! Other signs that are funny but really should be considered works of art include:

- A collection of three-inch-tall Wizard of Oz characters—Dorothy with her red shoes, the shiny Tin Man, the Wicked Witch on a bike, the Cowardly Lion, and the straw Scarecrow.
- A green car that has a popped-open trunk showing two-inch pieces of luggage. In the car are two happy iguanas, one with a fly on his tongue; dice swinging from the mirror; and detail that makes this look real, except downscaled in size!
- A spinning circus, with a man in a cannon, a lion tamer in a fancy white outfit, with a chair in one hand and a whip in the other to keep the lion at bay; an iguana wearing a pink tutu is swinging above, looking down on many other circus acts. All of this is contained under a canopy. Pretty incredible.

All three of those were created by the same couple, Andrea and Sal, and they usually either win the contest or place in the top three. It makes you wonder, though— how do they find time to dive?

The art contest has become so popular and well known that we actually have people who cycle up the road from another resort to check out the creations. It is unbelievable! And just when you think you've seen the best, the funniest, or the most realistic, yet another amazingly creative submission is entered in the contest. We've just started putting the contest on the website every January, so you can vote on your favorite.

For many people, Christmas is the hardest holiday to be here. Although we exchange gifts, there is a tinge of sadness ... your original family is far away, but since this is one of the busiest times, most of us have not been "home" at Christmas in years. But some holiday events have made Little Cayman an enjoyable substitute. The whole island has a sing-song, complete with white-bearded Santa Claus in a tropical red outfit, passing out brightly colored and beribboned presents for the few kids on the island. (As of this writing, there are nine school kids.) Carols are sung in the huge, gorgeous new church donated by Capt. Charles Kirkconnell. Last year's caroling had homeowners, resort guests, and workers totaling 168 people! I remember the first year we did the Christmas caroling ... we piled into the back of a pickup truck and drove by the three resorts with everyone singing, badly out of tune, as I played on a portable keyboard. On the stage of the new church is a beautiful black baby grand Kawai piano, purchased with contributions from me and other members of the community. We even formed a twelve-member choir, complete with robes, to sing for Christmas, Easter, and the grand opening of the church. We've come a long way for an island with just a little over a hundred residents.

After the sing-song, Gladys hosts an open house at the resort. The whole clubhouse is turned into a wall-to-wall buffet table. The heavenly smells of homemade breads and desserts fill the air, and red bows and garlands decorate the windows. Twinkling white lights adorn the walkways, and a beautifully decorated tree with ornaments from around the world brings a feeling of gratitude for Christmas and for friends on the island. Roasted hams, smoked turkeys, and smoked salmon (all hand-carried in!) are laid out near homemade mayonnaise and fresh-baked rolls. Coconut shrimp with caribe dipping sauce, pasta salad, spinach balls, caviar pie, artichoke-mushroom dip, and other gourmet delights entice us. Sorrel punch, both with and without alcohol, gives the meal a Caribbean flair.

Once you're stuffed, you realize there's another whole room full of desserts! The dessert room has decorated trays laden with homemade fruitcake, chocolate fudge, rum balls, pralines, powdered crescent cookies, peanut-butter brownies, banana-mango cheesecake, and white chocolate–cranberry biscotti. Yummmm ... who's counting calories? This is always the favorite room, if you have space left on your plate—or in your stomach.

After everyone is sated and content, the hilarious gag gift exchange begins, leaving everyone with a smile. Everyone has been told to bring an inexpensive, funny gift to exchange—the funnier, the better. Where do they *find* some of these gifts? The gift exchange, of course, is led by "Santa" Gladys. The first person picks a gift and opens it. The second person can trade for the first gift or choose an unopened one. The third guy can trade for any of the opened gifts or choose a new one ... on and on it goes until everyone has some silly gift. The reason it becomes so funny is that certain items become favorite choices that *everybody* wants! When it's your turn, you can trade three times, then Gladys blows a whistle—and you are stuck with your funny tie, mermaid-handled coffee mug, seashell candle, funky hat, wind-up toy, or whatever. One year, for some reason, all the items had a sexual connotation. Of course, this was the same year that a visiting Brac preacher, his wife, and their kids came to join us … *uh-oh!* We had not asked them to bring gifts, so Gladys and I scrambled around the beach and wrapped doll legs, conch shells, and whatever else we could find—quickly. As the gift exchange began and people realized the "theme", everyone began glancing at the visitors to see how they were taking the subject matter—a plastic sheep with orifices, a deck of cards featuring scantily clad women, a book on how to keep your relationship *alive!*, etc. The preacher's wife's turn finally came, and she chose to open … a Chip-n-Dale's beefcake calendar! You should have seen her ogle Mr. April! Mr. December was all wrapped up and ready to go … what a hoot! She would *not* let go of the calendar, either. No one could or would trade for it after a while … let her be … It's a lot of fun, and most people end up with what they want—or at least they walk home with a funny gift and a smile on their face. A good time is always had by all.

11

How to Live on an Island: Anonymous Words of Wisdom

1. Always, always, *always* double-check everything.
2. Remember, you are on *their* time—island time.
3. You must have satellite TV.
4. Learn to expect curveballs—then you can deal with anything.
5. We are all playing at wannabe recluses.
6. It's an island of misfit toys.
7. Keep your sense of humor.
8. *Accept* the fact that everything is done on island time.
9. Don't Stop the Carnival.
10. As the island turns, so do the days of your lives.
11. Islands are magnets for flotsam and jetsam—human and otherwise. Love it or leave.
12. My only job is to watch the waves come in and out, and make sure they keep coming in and out ... in and out ...
13. You know you are Caymanized when you stand in the water, drinking your Heineken, finish it, fill the bottle with water, turn it over, let it spill out, fill it with water, turn it over, let it spill out, fill it ... (no

agenda).

14. Learn to make do with what you have.
15. Living on an island—if you're not half crazy when you move there, you'll go absolutely nuts!
16. Be prepared to have everyone see your dirty laundry.
17. A sense of humor is crucial, and you can't get too caught up with things.
18. Ya gotta do what ya gotta do, on a small island.
19. Hip-deep in the sea, with a drink in one hand and a fishing pole in the other, staring blankly at the water ... "Beauty is everywhere; you just have to look."
20. Paradise with restrictions.
21. Learn to be a handyperson because if you have a problem or need to get something fixed or done, you either do it yourself or accept "no problem, soon come".
22. The first year you work in Little Cayman, it's about the adventure. By the second year, you're here for the money. By the third year, you're here because you don't know how to fit in anywhere else anymore.
23. Never a dull moment.
24. Why should I work in this hot sun, when the breadfruit is ripe ... and the conch can't run?
25. A stay of longer than ten days allows local politics to catch you.
26. If it's going to break or rust, it's gonna do it in Little Cayman.
27. You have to *really* want to be here, because it's not easy in paradise.
28. Know when to say something and when to stay

quiet.

29. Be prepared to wait three times as long and pay three times as much.
30. Best to stay off the drinking merry-go-round.
31. "Island fever" or "rock fever" is real. If you're living here full time, it's important to go back "home" periodically for a reality check.

12

A Little Caymanian History

As I was finishing up the stories in this book, the Cayman Islands were celebrating their five-hundred-year history. I know when I travel, I enjoy knowing a bit about a place, so this chapter was created to share with you some "fun facts". It's by no means complete, but it was fun interviewing some of the island people who were actually a part of this history, and could remember the events!

The Cayman Islands have some of the friendliest people around—there are no unemployed (unless they want to be), so no beggars or street people trying to hustle the tourists. It has a safe, old-fashioned, friendly environment, and that's why people return over and over again. There is a melting pot of various nationalities—English, Irish, Honduran, American, Canadian, Jamaican, and others. The islands are just south of Cuba, and are actually the peaks of submerged mountains. But since we are wanting to know what was here *before* tourism and all these cultural blends, we'll take a look at history. How did people survive before stores and civilization? I hope you find some of this information as entertaining as I did—it sure makes me appreciate what we have today.

Fun Facts from Sam McCoy

Common name	Local name
Caribbean birch	Tourist tree (red and peeling)
West Indian Whistling-Duck	Whistling duck
Blackbird, Grackle	Ching-ching
Black-billed Ani	Blacksmith, Old Arnold
Filefish	Press bag
Butterfly fish	Four-eye fish
Minnows	Fry
Horse-eyed jack	Crevalle
Kingfish	Wahoo
Surgeonfish	Doctorfish
Deepwater grouper	Day grouper
Bottlenose dolphin	Pampose
Scorpionfish	Numbfish
Black durgeon	Prop-prop
Coney	Butterfish
Octopus	Sea cat
Sea urchin	Sea egg

MORE FUN FACTS

The following information comes from the Cayman Islands National Museum, the Cayman Islands National Archive, the magazines *Key to Cayman* and *Cayman Horizons*, Ed Ritch, Sam McCoy, and John Mulak.

NATIONAL TREE

The silver thatch palm was used long ago as roofing material for the early settlers' simple wattle and daub cottages. The leaves were also woven to make hats and baskets, and when twisted together, made the best salt-resistant rope, which was used by Jamaican as well as Caymanian fishermen and turtlers. Silver thatch (*Coccothrinax proctorii*) is found only in the Cayman Islands.

NATIONAL BIRD

The Grand Cayman Parrot, a subspecies of the Cuban Parrot, has green feathers, a white crown, and red cheeks. They roost in palm stumps and mangroves at dusk. The Cayman Brac parrot, which looks slightly different, is one of the rarest Amazon parrots in the world.

NATIONAL FLOWER

The wild banana orchid comes in two varieties. The Grand Cayman variety is white with purple tips, whereas the Sister Islands variety is yellow with purple tips. The best time to see these orchids in flower is after the rains in May and June.

NATIONAL SYMBOL

The green sea turtle was found in great abundance around the Cayman Islands many years ago and was an integral part of the islands' history. They are still fairly abundant today and are seen quite often in the wild, though they are listed as an endangered species worldwide. Turtle fishing is very restricted in order to protect them. All of the dive areas are marine parks.

CAYMANIAN MOTTO

"He hath founded it upon the seas" (from Psalm 24).

LANGUAGE

The official language is English, though the local dialects, which differ between islands and even between districts, can be hard to understand at first. The intonations and pronunciations have been influenced by Scottish, Irish, Welsh, southern American, and Jamaican English.

In the earliest days of settlement, the people lived off the land and the sea. Their protein, or "meatkind", came from the sea—fish, turtle, conch, lobster, whelk. On small plantations, or "provision grounds", they grew starchy vegetables and tubers such as sweet potatoes, yams, and cassava. They also grew sugar cane and ground it on hand mills to get cane syrup, which they would boil down until it became sugar. Their salt came from holes in the limestone where seawater would accumulate and then evaporate, leaving the salt. They made starch for cooking and porridge for eating out of cassava and bulrush, and drank tea made from lemon grass ("fever grass"), basil, and mint. They rendered their own coconut oil and used it for cooking and for treating the hair. They drank the coconut water and grated the meat to make coconut milk. Everything was cooked on the caboose, which was kept in a separate building or shed called the cookroom, away from the house to avoid smoke and fire.

HISTORICAL TIMELINE

1503   Christopher Columbus's crew were the first people to record the Cayman Islands. The uninhabited Sister Islands were sighted and called Las Tortugas, meaning "the turtles". Columbus's son, Ferdinand, wrote in the log: "we sighted two very small low islands full of turtles (as was all the sea thereabout, so that it seemed to be full of little rocks)".

1526 A map made by Juan Vespucci gave these islands the name "Caymanos" and showed their position in the Caribbean reasonably accurately. *Caymanos* was derived from the Carib Indian word for crocodile. Crocodiles were plentiful here at the time of discovery, though some think the reference could be to the native iguanas.

1586 Sir Francis Drake's fleet of twenty-three ships stopped in Grand Cayman for two days. Soldiers reported seeing no people but plenty of crocodiles, alligators, iguanas, and turtles.

1660s The first settlers arrived in Little Cayman and Cayman Brac. They left the islands for Grand Cayman within a few years.

1669 The Spanish privateer Manuel Rivero Pardal attacked and seized English ships at Little Cayman and burned the twenty or so turtlers' huts on the island. This event probably was the origin of the legend of a pirate attack at Bloody Bay.

1670 Under the Treaty of Madrid, Spain ceded to England all the Caribbean islands that were already occupied by England. Although uninhabited, the Cayman Islands were included due to their proximity to Jamaica, claimed by England in 1662.

1700 Loggers, fisherman, and provision planters began establishing permanent settlements on Grand Cayman. Privateers and even pirates were frequent visitors until about 1730.

1730 The Spanish brigantine *San Miguel*, transporting

foodstuffs and merchandise from Spain to her colonies, plowed into Little Cayman's reef. All but four of the crew were lost. The English pirate Neal Walker plundered the vessel's cargo of fresh fruit and barrels of brandy and wine. Ballast stones, cannon, and anchors from the wreck can be seen under Little Cayman's waters. (Today, shipwrecks are protected by law, as part of our maritime history.)

1740s The principal industries were turtling, export of mahogany and logwood to Jamaica, shipbuilding, and ropemaking.

1773 The first accurate map of Cayman was made by Royal Navy hydrographer George Gauld. The population was about 450, half free and half slaves.

1800s Canoes were used to get around between the islands. The canoe was made from a single tree, preferably the cotton tree from Jamaica, and was twenty-six to twenty-eight feet long with a five-foot beam. The boats were propelled by rowing.

1831 Little Cayman was surveyed by Royal Navy surveyor Richard Owen, aboard HMS *Blossom*, who made the first official hydrographic survey of the Sister Islands. Few place names appeared on his chart.

1833 The first permanent settlements were established on Cayman Brac and Little Cayman. Cayman Brac was the more populous settlement because it had more and better land for plantations of yams, potatoes, cassava, plantain, banana, and sweet potatoes. Little Cayman's voracious iguanas would eat anything people planted.

1881 HMS *Sparrowhawk* brought a survey team to Little Cayman. Lt. Carpenter named Owen Island for Richard Owen, who made the 1831 survey, and Blossom Village after his ship. Sparrowhawk Hill, on the north side of Little Cayman, was probably named for Lt. Carpenter's vessel.

1885 The Carib Guano Company opened a phosphate mining operation in Little Cayman. Mined from deposits of decomposed bird droppings, phosphate was a valuable component of fertilizer. Mules were used to pull railroad carts full of phosphate to Salt Rocks, where the waiting ships would turn stern to shore and load the cargo across. The mule pen and tramway have been preserved, next to the Nature Trail. Eventually the phosphate was depleted. The coconut industry flourished for a while, with as many as a million coconuts being exported annually, until a blight killed off most of the trees.

1892 *Maggie E. Gray*, a Baltimore schooner engaged in phosphate shipping, wrecked off Little Cayman. It is believed that the boat was anchored and the wind changed direction, causing the schooner to strike the shore. The anchor and rigging are visible on the reef.

Early 1900s Shipping was a major industry. Turtle shells were being shipped to Japan and England and coconuts to Jamaica, and staples such as flour were being brought back to Cayman.

1904 Capt. Daniel Jervis, a turtling captain from Cayman Brac, built the *Terror*, a short, wide planked boat that was more maneuverable than a canoe. Propelled by a foremounted sail and oars, it was the first Cayman catboat, designed for turtling. Catboats were fourteen feet long and three and a half feet wide, and were made from the wood of plopnut or mahogany trees. They became the distinctive Caymanian vessel and a symbol of Caymanian ingenuity and craftsmanship.

1920   A small boat-repair business was taking place in Little Cayman's sound. Boats were pulled up to the beach for repair. The community grew to about 125 people—Foster, Hunter, Wood, Bodden, and Ritch were the names of some of these families.

1932   The terrible hurricane remembered as the Storm of '32 killed 108 Brackers. Although no lives were lost in Little Cayman, the population dwindled to fifty or sixty. Families started drifting away, moving to the U.S. and Jamaica looking for work. When men were lost at sea, the women and children left behind often left to join their families in order to survive.

1933   A small wooden church was built on a small rise of land just outside the village in Little Cayman. In later years, this church held as many as seventy-five people for Easter and Christmas services, and chairs were set outside for extra seating. The church is still standing and is considered a historic monument.

1952   The amphibious Catalina *Santa Maria* became the first airplane to land on an airstrip in the

Cayman Islands.

1954 Community volunteers built an airstrip on Cayman Brac.

1958 Dr. Logan Robertson started the Southern Cross Club as a private fishing camp, consisting first of tents, then, in the 1970s, wooden buildings. It was the first resort on Little Cayman.

1960 Motorboats began to replace "Norwegian steam power", or oars, for local use. The number of people living on Little Cayman had dwindled to ten—owners of a few private homes and a "me-one" (single-owner) shop. Ed Ball built his experimental home here.

1962 Edward Bodden Airfield on Little Cayman was built with private funds.

1971 Faith Hospital, another community initiative, was opened on Cayman Brac.

1976 The *Soto Trader*, a steel-hulled inter-island freighter carrying propane and gasoline for Cayman Brac and Little Cayman, burned while dispensing fuel. Fumes collected in the hold and were ignited by a spark, and flames engulfed the vessel. Most of the crew escaped. The *Soto Trader* sank in sixty feet of water with a cargo of cement mixers and trucks, which are visible on dives today.

1973 The Ritches' house was built in Little Cayman.

1980s When houses were first being built on Little Cayman, workers were imported from Cayman Brac and boarded on Little Cayman during the week. On weekends, they would travel back to the Brac to stay with their families. Government workers were rotated in and out, and joked about their "prison sentence" on Little Cayman. Some of the first non-Caymanian couples who came to Little Cayman to build homes and lives, when it could take an hour to drive to the village on the rugged road, were John and B.J. Mulak, Basil and Brigitte Kassa, Ron and Nancy Sefton, and Charlie and Genevieve Robbins. During the 1980s, a sanitary landfill was opened and the road began to be paved, a small section at a time. At some point in the mid-1980s, a wrecked boat and a small aircraft that had experienced engine problems were on either side of the airstrip to greet guests as they landed on Little Cayman.

1981   The Southern Cross Club shut down. Thirty-two shareholders bought it and brought in managers, including Mike Emmanuelle and John and Marilyn Palmer.

1983   Queen Elizabeth II was the first reigning monarch to visit the Cayman Islands, accompanied by her husband, Prince Philip, Duke of Edinburgh.

1986   Gladys Howard, from Tyler, Texas, bought Pirates Point Resort, which was Logan Robertson's home in the 1970s. John Palmer's house was built on Little Cayman. In the absence of a concrete mixer, all cement had to be mixed by hand.

1987   Sam and Mary McCoy opened McCoy's Lodge, beginning with two rooms and eventually expanding into a ten-room resort. The Cayman Islands Government created a marine park system with moorings, so that boats wouldn't anchor in the coral, and protected areas of the marine environment by limiting the amount of conch, lobster, and fish that can be taken from each area. (The marine park, which is where the divers are most of the time, is a "No take" zone.) *Carrie Lee,* a cargo boat bringing lumber for Ray and Betty Van Culin's house in Little Cayman and tar for the road, capsized in Grand Cayman because it was overloaded.

1988   Hurricane Gilbert, with 110-mph winds, caused the few residents and guests to seek shelter in an airport hangar. We heard on a portable radio that there were "no known survivors". Gilbert took out a Brac landmark, Ottley Scott's Coral Isle Club on the south side. Pirates Point Resort lost one generator and had to re-roof. There was water damage to the rooms, and lots of tree debris, but we could open back up. Southern Cross Club had three feet of sand in each room, and it was a month before they could accept guests again.

1990   The designation "Lesser Islands" for Cayman Brac and Little Cayman was discontinued and replaced with "Sister Islands". The small wooden church on Little Cayman was renovated and re-opened. The island's generator-operated electrical plant began service to some parts of Little Cayman. The section of road by Point of Sand was added onto, thus completing the road around the island.

1991   Cayman Brac Power & Light began operations in Little Cayman.

1992   Village Square, containing a grocery store and gas station, was opened in Little Cayman.

1993   Little Cayman's first Mardi Gras parade was held. Prince Charles and his party visited Little Cayman on the Royal Yacht *Britannia* and had a picnic at Owen Island.

1995   Peter Hillenbrand bought Southern Cross Club and began major renovations. The power plant began service to the north coast of Little Cayman. Pirates Point and a few private homes still have generators, just in case. The first policeman, Bob Freemantle, and his wife, Janet, came to live in Little Cayman.

1996   The National Trust building on Little Cayman was built and dedicated by Governor Gore. The island's first parsonage was built.

1997   After torrential rains from a tropical storm, tarpon were seen swimming in the roads. A rescue effort returned eighty-four tarpon safely to the pond. Mike Lewis became the first Marine Enforcement Officer to live on Little Cayman and work with the people toward protecting the marine parks and marine life. Nancy Norman became the first full-time nurse to live and work on Little Cayman. Dan and Kathy Shroy and their children, Caroline and Matt, became the first full-time preacher and family to live on Little Cayman.

1998   The house owned by actor Burgess Meredith (better known as Penguin) was renovated. Hurricane Mitch demolished all the docks on the south side of Little Cayman. They were rebuilt within a month of the storm. House numbers came to the island, and street lights were installed (to mixed response).

1999   After a short spurt of growth, thirty-five houses and condos were for sale.

2000   Street name signs were installed, generating some island talk about how the names were chosen. A police station was opened—and has had some overnight "guests".

2002   Capt. Charles Kirkconnell donated the land and building for a huge new church. A grand opening drew a large crowd, including the Governor. Members of the community raised funds to purchase a baby grand piano for the church.

2003   The Cayman Islands celebrated its Quincentennial, marking five hundred years since its discovery. The Maritime Heritage Trail project was launched, with interpretive signs marking the sites of shipwrecks from as early as 1730 to the present day. Prince Edward came to cut the ribbon on a historical monument in Little Cayman's Blossom Village park. More than four hundred engraved brick pavers created a walkway surrounding the monument. The National Trust and the community hosted an afternoon tea for the Prince. The Cayman Islands passed a law to ban the fishing of spawning grouper for eight years—an attempt to allow the grouper the chance to reproduce enough to keep the spawning aggregation from vanishing forever.

Today, Little Cayman's Bloody Bay wall is one of the world's top five dive destinations. Since the wall drops off six thousand feet and more, the visibility is always great. You never know what you might see next ... The island is also explored for indigenous flora and fauna, including wild iguanas, West Indian Whistling-Ducks, and other varied bird life, including the largest colony of Red-footed Boobies in the Western Hemisphere.

Five hundred years after its discovery, this island has been re-discovered ... and developed. What is its future? It does not have unlimited resources, and once something precious is gone, there is no going back. This book was written partly as a collection of funny stories, and partly in the hope of letting people know what a special place Little Cayman is. It is unique ... and I'm glad I have lived a great part of my life here and could share some of the funny stories with you. We hope to see you on our island, and would love to welcome you to our unique and wonderful resort, Pirates Point.

Afterword and Acknowledgments

When I started thinking of writing the Acknowledgments page, the list of names kept growing. Plus, I'm afraid of leaving anyone out ... I could say thanks to everyone I've met in life, and that would cover it all! Actually, that's true, because everyone whom I have met has in some way touched my life. That seems more true as I get older—even "bad" experiences happened for a reason.

When I first thought of writing a book, I received a lot of encouragement from past Pirates Point guests whom I need to thank. I think they just wanted to see their name or stories in print! Thanks to all of you!

The biggest lesson I learned doing this book is something my dad used to tell me: everyone has a story to tell, if we learn to listen. We also have to learn to listen to our "gut". People kept telling me to write the book, and a couple of events told me to do it too. One night at about 3:00 a.m. I woke from a deep sleep with the thought "I *should* write this book." I went downstairs, grabbed a big spiral notebook, and started writing—and about a year later, it's all coming together. The next event was when I was thinking, "I need to find an illustrator."

You've read about the Easter auction; well, that same day, looking at the items in the auction, I saw an artist's work that was bright Caribbean colors and *fun*! I returned to the resort, and there was a lady in the bar, finding a book to read. I started excitedly saying, "I love this artwork ..." and described it, and said, "I would love to have it for my book," and she said, "That's my work—and I would *love* to illustrate your book!" Thank you, Judy Steele! Judy well knows what it's like to live on an island: she lived on Grand Cayman for twelve years, where she was the political cartoonist for the islands' newspaper, the *Caymanian Compass*.

Then, about a year later, when I had written most of the stories, I woke up thinking, "I need to find an editor." In to work I go, that same day, and a woman from the Brac was finishing breakfast and reading a book. Everyone else had come and gone already, so it was a bit unusual—she was there by herself. We started talking about books, sharing our love of reading. I said, "I'm writing a book," and she said she would like to read it ... Not having a lot of confidence in whether it was even worth letting someone read, I loaned her my spiral notebook. The next day, I mentioned that I was in search of an editor ... and she said, "That's what I do, and I would *love* to edit it for you ...". Thank you, Claudette Upton! Claudette recently edited a major new history of the Cayman Islands, *Founded upon the Seas*, which was published in late 2003.

Kathleen Doler, another editor and friend, had additional input. She is an inspiration to me. Ron Carlisle and Tim Boyd are the guys "behind the scenes" who are helping to make this venture work. Thanks, too, to Jeff Anderson for the photo of me on the back cover.

Other island people who helped with the history were Ed and Madge Ritch—Ed should be writing a history book! John Mulak provided notes of interest for the time-line, and I also am grateful to John and B.J. for sharing their enthusiasm for life on a small island.

If I had to thank anyone *first*, it would be the women who brought me to the Cayman Islands. Bitsy Henderson and Laura Robinson, y'all brought me here and gave me the chance to live my dream! Thank you.

Don Foster gave me my first Caribbean job—but more than that, he catered to people and showed them how to have fun diving ... one of my mentors.

My mother and dad, Margaret and Floyd Cokendolpher, and my brother, Larry, were my beginning. My love to all of you, but I had the travel bug early! Another mentor from early in my life before diving was my piano teacher, Edie Crockett. She taught me a love of music and we developed a close bond that I have always treasured.

Credit for my early diving years goes to J. Rich Sports and all the neat people who made it happen. They created a safe, fun environment and a very thorough dive course. I'm proud to have been part of the team. Thanks to Jim Fuller, Peter Oliver, Paul Johnston, Ron Carlisle, Stephanie Scott, and Jim Bowden. I'm especially thankful for reconnecting with a beautiful person and friend, Karen Hohle.

To my fellow workers at the resort, who make it so much fun: Peter, Steve, Dianne, Cam, and Valda, and all the past and future workers—thanks. Coco and Martha get special mention because they're mentors not only in diving but also in life's little lessons. Thank you for the enjoyable hours above and below water. Coco's my fellow seahorse finder, and Martha is a sweetheart (Texas talk!) and my inspiration as I strive for peace and serenity.

I saved the best for last—Gladys Howard stands in a class by herself. Those who know her know what I mean. There are not enough words to thank Gladys. We've been through it all together—births, deaths, laughter, tears, highs and lows. It has never been boring, and I've enjoyed working with and for such a fun lady. The guests are always first with us. I value the knowledge I have gained and am proud of what we have all created together.

Another person who has an infectious love of life, and with whom I spent many happy, close years, was my original dive buddy, Danny Self. Some of my fondest memories before Pirates Point are of Danny.

My life at Pirates Point includes an additional person—my husband, Ed. He has provided a wonderfully stable home life that has helped me grow as a person. Whatever I have gone through, he has been supportive. The stories HE could tell ... if only I would let him!

One last story to end the book ...

My girlfriend Karen and Jim Bowden are both well traveled and can blend in just about anywhere they go ... or so they thought! One of their trips was to a *very* remote part of Mexico. In fact, as they stopped off for a beer, they realized that this bar was definitely not on any tourist map! They *like* to travel where the locals go ... good spots to eat, drink, and see the non-tourist side of a country. As they walked into the bar, there was this great Spanish music playing. As she sat down to order a Mexican *cerveza*, she noticed the music had changed to Tom Jones, and the bartender brought over two Budweisers! Oh well, as I said in the beginning, we are all tourists, anytime we visit a new place.

I hope this book has left you with some happy thoughts for traveling. In these uncertain times, with airport security making travel a bit more troublesome, just remember: You don't need much but a change of clothes and a good sense of humor to have a fun vacation, wherever you go!

Glossary of Useful Terms

BC or buoyancy compensator. A flotation jacket to help keep a scuba diver floating on the surface of the water. It is also used underwater to help a diver maintain his position at the desired depth. Air is added to or removed from the jacket to achieve natural buoyancy at any given depth.

breath-hold diving. A dive on lung power. The diver fully inflates his or her lungs and dives underwater without the use of scuba gear. Some people train to increase the time and depth they can achieve underwater.

buoyancy. Where the diver is in the water column. Negative buoyancy means on the bottom. Positive buoyancy is floating up or on top of the water. Neutral buoyancy is being able to swim mid-water, neither floating up nor sinking down. This is what divers want to achieve when diving.

C card. A scuba diver's certification card, which shows proof of diving credentials.

depth limits. Divers are required to stay at certain depths for safety reasons, depending on their skill, experience, and training level. Novice divers have to stay between 0 and 60 feet. The depth limits for the Cayman Islands and for experienced divers are 60 to

100 feet. The absolute depth limits for sport divers are 100 to 130 feet. Below 130 feet, dive at your own risk.

drydock. Dive boats are pulled out of the water and put into a marina for yearly maintenance. Typically, the bottom is painted—and this paint sometimes rubs off on snorkelers who get too close to the boat!

mask. A contoured face plate and plastic rim that provides an air space so our eyes can see underwater. Our nose is also enclosed so that, as divers, we can equalize water pressure as we descend underwater.

mooring. In the Cayman Islands, a mooring is a core coral piece drilled out of the bottom, with a line put into the hole and cemented into place. Boats attach to these permanent moorings instead of throwing an anchor into the living coral. The moorings were created to help save the reef from repeated anchor damage.

nitrogen narcosis. As divers go underwater, their bodies absorb nitrogen in the bloodstream from the air they are breathing. At depth, some divers become "narced" as a result of the nitrogen. It is similar to feeling drunk, uncaring or unconcerned. The effects disappear as soon as the diver reaches shallower water.

nor'wester. In the Cayman Islands, this is our winter storm. High winds come from the northwest, creating huge waves splashing the shoreline. Nor'westers usually last only a couple of days, but have been known to hang around for a *long* week.

no-see-ums. A tiny biting insect that comes out just as the sun sets. You never see 'em, but you sure feel 'em. For sunset watching, spray up with Off or wear long pants!

pi_a colada. A favorite tourist drink, created to give you
the feeling of being in the islands—rum, pi_a colada
mix, pineapple juice, and ice in the blender. You can
add a little umbrella if you really want to go all the
way! Remember, if you want to look like a local, skip
the pi_a colada and drink the rum straight or with
Coca-Cola.

regulator hoses. To go underwater, a diver has a regulator to regulate the air from the scuba tank to the
diver's mouth. On the regulator is also a spare, or
"octopus", mouthpiece that the diver's buddy can
breathe on, if necessary. Another hose has a pressure
gauge, like the gas gauge on a car, telling how much
air is in the scuba tank. The last hose attaches to the
BC and can put air into the BC to adjust buoyancy.

safety bar/hang strap. A ten-foot-long bar, dropped off
a dive boat and hung at about fifteen feet. This is
where divers "hang" at the end of a dive to "outgas",
or get rid of nitrogen taken up on the dive.

sergeant major. A small striped fish abundant in the
Cayman Islands. It loves to follow snorkeling boats.

snorkel. A small tube that attaches to the mask. It allows
you to lie face down on the water and still breathe air.

"Soon come". A Caymanian phrase meaning be patient,
I (or whatever you're waiting for) will be there eventually.

tank strap. A strap that constitutes the back part of a BC
and holds the tank to the BC.

weight belt and weights. Divers need to wear weight on
a belt to get them underwater. The amount depends
on size, comfort, level of activity, and whether the

diver is wearing a wetsuit.

wetsuit. A body suit, short or full-length, usually made out of neoprene, that helps keep a diver warm underwater.

yellowtail snapper. A slender white fish with a yellow racing stripe and a yellow tail. He can be seen "racing" to the next piece of food being handed out by divers, and is known by the nickname "Cayman piranha".

About the Resort

After reading this book, you might want to come visit us—that is my hope, anyway. Remember, Little Cayman is a quiet, friendly community of only 125 people. There are no TVs or phones in the rooms at Pirates Point. Nature puts on an incredible show, and the resort has a wonderful ambience. If this sounds good to you, then come see us.

Pirates Point is truly a unique place to vacation. I have heard people say many times, "We never go back to the same place twice ..." and yet we see them again and again.

Check out our website:
www.piratespointresort.com
or call us at 1-345-948-1010
or fax us at 1-345-948-1011

You can also e-mail reservation requests to
piratept@candw.ky

Hope to see y'all real soon!

[Inside back cover]

[Author photo]

Gay Morse was born in south Texas and graduated from the University of Texas, Austin, with a degree in music education. She fell in love with scuba diving in 1980 when she took her first course, and began teaching in 1982. She has been a dive instructor in the Cayman Islands for almost twenty years. She lives in Little Cayman with her husband, Ed, and their cat, Cali. Gay would love to hear from readers, who can e-mail her at <eglit-cay@candw.ky>.

If you've enjoyed this book and want to order further copies, contact us at our e-mail address, <islandlife@scubadiving.com>. Our website is at www.islandslife.com.

If you're interested in Judy Steele's work, you can contact her by e-mail at <jbrownsteele@yahoo.com>.

For nature photos of Little Cayman, contact Jeff Anderson at <jeff.anderson@nature-imagery.com>.

1. No name attached. Many divemasters hear the call of the ocean floor (in Cayman that's thousands of feet deep!), and I don't want to get anyone in trouble.
2. Jim is the real name of a friend of mine who held the world record for deepest dive on scuba. He made the record on 6 April 1994 in Yucatan, Mexico; it has since been broken. This story did *not* happen to him, but I wanted to put his name in here in connection with deep diving.
3. Name changed because he moved on.
4. Name changed because she's left the island.
5. Name changed—she's moved on.
6. Name changed because she still wants to be able to work in the Islands!
7. Evidence of mental instability surfaced during the week.
8. Not his real name.
9. I made up her name, but the turtle story *is* true.
10. Name changed because he's related to someone we know.
11. Name changed to protect the irresponsible.
12. See previous note.
13. No longer on island.
14. Name changed to protect the gullible.
15. "Harry" has moved on.
16. If you're interested in more island recipes, Gladys Howard's cookbook, *Cook'in Little Cayman*, has some delicious favorites. The proceeds go to the National Trust. You can order it by fax at 1-345-948-1011 or by e-mail at <piratept@candw.ky>. We will need a check, and donations for island land conservation are gratefully accepted. We can give you all the information by fax. Thanks!
17. I'm unsure where "Susan" is today and couldn't get her permission to use her real name.
18. Name changed to protect his dance troupe back home.
19. Names changed to protect the perfectionist.
20. Name changed to protect the young and innocent.
21. Name changed to protect the hairless.
22. Name changed to protect the surgically enhanced.
23. Name changed because he is trying to start a new life.
24. Name changed, but we all know who he is.

25. She's no longer around to give permission for her real name to be used.
26. Names withheld because they don't want to go to jail.
27. This is his real name. He said I could use it. We know who does the pranks anyway!
28. Name changed because he was angry.
29. Name not changed. We know whose dock!
30. Name changed because he lives in Grand Cayman now.
31. Name changed to protect this "workaholic".
32. Names changed to protect the guilty.
33. Name changed to protect innocent Grandma.